What readers are saying:

"Read Ripple *and Chris's six principles with a highlighter and grab a pen
for the practical exercises to drive the principles home."*

R. Michael Rose, CEO of Mojo Media Labs and author of
ROE Powers ROI: The Ultimate Way to Think and Communicate for Ridiculous Results

*"Leadership begins internally, a service to self that if nurtured, can expand beyond you and allow
you to serve others.* Ripple *is the missing manual for this inside-out leadership—a book you can visit
to make a quick adjustment (there's even a 'But I Need Help Now!' section) or to begin a warm, step-
by-step mentorship with Chris. Finally, a leadership book not of rules, but of actions."*

Michael Clingan, The Claymore Group

"The principles outlined in Ripple *are not just sound business advice. They provide a springboard for
creativity in figuring out what kind of leader you are and how you can go from being a good leader
to an outstanding one. Highly original and truly engaging!"*

Marshall Goldsmith, a Thinkers50 Top Ten Global Business Thinker and top-ranked executive coach

*"Ripple reminds us that leadership starts with personal clarity and results in immeasurable impact.
The simple exercises in this book will help you learn to focus on your strengths, improve your
organization, and positively influence the lives of others."*

Marisa Smith, head brainiac, The Whole Brain Group

*"Having interviewed leaders of so many extraordinary companies in the United States, Japan, and
beyond, I can tell you with confidence that every organizational issue is a leadership issue. In other
words, if you want to change your organization, work on your leadership first!*

Many of us mistakenly believe that leadership is a talent that you are born with, but Ripple *shows
you that leadership can be learned. Throughout this easy-to-follow, entertaining book, Chris
Hutchinson provides you with exercises that help you cultivate a profound understanding of "self"
and empower you to make a far-reaching and lasting impact."*

Shinobu Ishizuka, author of *Zapposu No Kiseski (The Zappos Miracle)*

ripple

ripple

A FIELD MANUAL FOR LEADERSHIP THAT WORKS

Chris Hutchinson

lasting impact
PRESS

Ripple
Published by Lasting Impact Press
405 Mason Ct., Suite 113
Fort Collins, CO 80524

Cover and interior design by Launie Parry, Red Letter Creative
Interior illustrations by Chris Hutchinson
Edited by Karla Oceanak and Matthew Gardner

Library of Congress Cataloging-in-Publication Data

Hutchinson, Chris
Ripple: A Field Manual for Leadership That Works
by Chris Hutchinson.

ISBN: 978-1-942492-00-9

1. Business / leadership 2. Organizations / Organizational effectiveness
3. Success in business / mentoring & coaching

Printed in the United States of America
2015 - First Edition

Special Sales
For special quantity discounts for your corporation, organization, or special-interest group, please contact Lasting Impact Press at www.lastingimpactpress.com.

This book is in memory of my friend Brian Robins.

Fly away free, Brian.

I dedicate this book to my good friend Brian Wayne Robins. He and I went to school together at the University of Colorado in the mid-1980s. We met in AFROTC and Aerospace Engineering 101, and we spent long nights together eating pizza and solving programming problems in his dorm room. He introduced me to Day-Timers, which kept me organized and in school. I was honored to have him be part of my wedding with Diana in 1987, and Brian faithfully sent us anniversary cards for the rest of his life. During our Air Force careers, Brian and I got to work together a few times, notably when he flew me and a team I led into Albania in 1996. In 2005 he found the love of his life, Robyn, and Diana and I got to attend his wedding. He even tolerated some coaching from me around the great plans he had for his family and career. In 2011 he discovered that he had advanced brain cancer and passed away a short time later, on 6 November. Robyn and their son, Greg, are a very special connection to Brian for our whole family, and he is missed.

Contents

Preface

Right now you're likely trying to decide if you really want to spend your time and energy reading this book.

Here's why you should:

If you believe there is more capacity in you, in others, and in your organization than is now being tapped, this book is worth it.

Why? Because it's built to help you:

- Self-identify what's working and what's not so you can quickly focus effort where it's needed;

- Build your confidence and effectiveness working with people at all levels of your organization; and

- Create practical solutions to your current challenges while strengthening your ability to handle future challenges.

In the past two decades, I've worked with hundreds of organizations and thousands of leaders and leaders-in-training. Some were amazingly effective, while others struggled to make the right things happen. The biggest differences between those who succeeded and those who struggled were:

- Their understanding of their strengths and what they wanted to achieve;

- Their willingness to challenge themselves and learn; and

- Their ability to put their learning into action.

This book helps people like you achieve greater and longer-lasting success in less time. Here's to you getting as far as you want to go.

Note: throughout the book I share many client stories. Out of respect for the privacy of the people and organizations involved, some stories have identifying details changed.

Introduction

You can become a better leader by using the proven concepts in this book to improve your personal impact on your organization and the people who make it work.

It doesn't matter if you are a frontline supervisor, a mid-level manager, or a CEO. It doesn't matter if you are relatively new to leadership or a seasoned veteran. What does matter is that you must be willing to shift your awareness, learn some new tools, and do some challenging work.

How to dodge a silver bullet

Right now, the results you are getting are the best you can do considering the circumstances. Yet you wouldn't be reading this unless you believed things could be better. And there are at least two significant challenges standing between you and success.

The first challenge is your own personal awareness. Through no fault of your own, you are highly likely to be unaware of:

How you are contributing to situations, and

How to do things differently to make a difference.

How you are contributing to situations

This lack of awareness is fostered by things outside your control—such as the fact that people rarely tell leaders when their behavior is helping or hurting the team. Even when you are aware of how you're impacting others, everything is changing so quickly that it is extremely hard to predict what needs to happen next.

The second challenge is that today's organizational climate is creating unprecedented pressure to:

- **Do more with less**
- **Go faster, and**
- **Make no mistakes.**

How to do things differently to make a difference

These leadership challenges and pressures may cause you to seek rescue from a "silver bullet" or "magic pill"—something that will solve all your problems instantly without effort. Or, you may put yourself and your organization into permanent overdrive, leading to poor results, waste of resources, and burnout of everyone—including you.

Enter the Ripple effect

Don't fall prey to the false hope of the silver bullet. Instead, unleash the ripple effect.

This is a book of tested models and exercises you can use to self-diagnose and improve your skills quickly. It's a field guide that captures lessons you probably didn't learn in school yet are critical for thriving in the real world.

I've spent the last five years assembling and refining a simple framework of the most important principles affecting leaders' success, along with the effective practices supporting these principles. These principles and practices reflect the best research, field-testing, and refinement from all my work and my company's work with clients. In each practice, I include straightforward exercises to help you get started leveraging your organization, your team, and yourself to greater success.

Why this book?

Ever since I started my business, clients have asked me, "What one book should I use to work on my leadership?"

I read widely and have even been accused of being a "bibliotherapist." My library shelves include almost 20 linear feet of leadership books, ranging in focus from personal leadership to teamwork to organizational development.

If only for my clients, I wrote this book to provide something different, something that touched on the three areas critical to effective leadership:

- Personal effectiveness, self-knowledge, and internal direction
- Interpersonal communication, relationships, and employee development
- Organizational structure, direction, and systems improvement

This book is different because it builds a bridge between proven concepts and powerful ways to get things done in the real world. This book gives you tools and techniques then frees you to do things your way.

To help you succeed, this book incorporates three primary methods of communication:

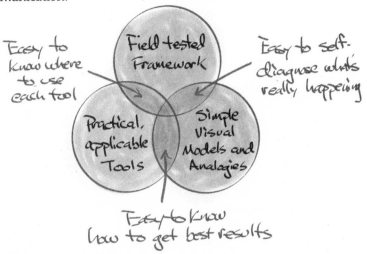

A field-tested framework of challenges leaders most often face

I've developed the concepts and practices in this book over a more than 20 year career as a leader and leadership coach. They will help you self-diagnose what's going right and what's going wrong, and see how you can personally make changes to get people and an organization back on track.

Visual models and analogies that make the concepts easy to grasp

This book has simple illustrations and stories that help you quickly understand "what good looks like." They create ideas that stick in your mind, so you can easily recall guidance when you need it.

Easy-to-use tools that break through resistance

This book is filled with real-life, practical solutions to the kinds of problems leaders like you face most. The exercises make it easy to get started and build positive momentum.

A new framework

This book pulls together proven concepts into a simple six-part framework of powerful ways to get things done. This framework is about helping you understand and drive yourself to action, how you connect with and empower people, and how you build and run an organization. These six principles are the essence of effective, influential leadership.

Principle 1 | **Leaders' effectiveness is proportional to how well they know themselves.**
As a state of being, deep self-alignment is the foundation for a leader's potential impact.

Principle 2 | **Leaders are judged more by what they don't than by what they do.**
As leader, no one will force you to do the things that matter — and neither will they forget if you don't.

Principle 3 | **People discover their best selves through being respected by a leader.**
Leaders who listen, look for, and uncover others' strengths create capacity and commitment.

Principle 4 | **People multiply a leader's power only as much as that power is shared.**
The success of a leader is determined by how much he or she can positively enable others.

Principle 5 | **Organizations are designed to get the results they are getting.**
Want different results? Design a different organization.

Principle 6 | **Organizations generating waste are generating opportunities for improvement.**
Lead the organization to minimize waste and optimize output.

Leveraging these six principles is not as complicated as most people believe — yet more challenging to do well than most people know. In other words, it's simple but not easy.

Start here

This section introduces you to the fundamentals of Ripple Leadership. Your re-orientation begins now.

A different mindset about leadership

Shooting marbles

Many people act as though leadership is an action you simply do and complete. As a leader your goal is to make things happen, like in a game of marbles. So you pick the biggest shooter marble you can find, figure out which marbles you want to move where, aim, and fire. The other marbles react upon impact. If they're good marbles they move to the locations you envisioned and stay there. And since you've exerted your authority, your job as leader is done.

The shooter-marble view of leadership might sound nice in theory, but it doesn't work in practice. People don't like being manipulated, and if they feel you are treating them like objects, you will inspire either outright rebellion, or the more insidious, unseen withdrawal of effort and resulting organizational ineffectiveness. People aren't marbles.

Skipping stones

The reality is that leadership is much more fluid, like skipping stones in a pond. It's more about influence and enabling the right things to happen rather than lining up a shot and "making it happen." You take a smooth stone, throw it at the proper angle, and marvel at the effect it makes as it glances off the water, creating ripples each time it hits the surface. That energy spreads out in all directions, reflecting off obstacles and edges, ideally making the right kinds of things happen. After a short while the surface becomes calm again, and it's time to skip another stone. Or in the case of leadership, it's time to use your influence again. The job of an effective leader never ends; it merely repeats and is refined over time.

The distinction between shooting marbles and skipping stones may seem small. It's not. It's huge. In fact, it's everything.

Leaders with the marble-game mindset are always looking for bigger shooters and new tricks to improve their shooting accuracy. They aim to win by knocking others out of the circle. Their goal is to directly impact others to make them comply and then stay where they want them.

In contrast, leaders with the skipping-stones mindset are always looking for the right shape of stone, checking out the surface of the water, and trying to see how many skips they can make. Their goal is to spread their influence as far as possible to cause the greatest good. And they know that their influence will fade and need to be replenished regularly.

> Here's the secret of leadership:
> The power to influence isn't in the stone.
> It's in the ripples.

Ripples interact, sometimes canceling each other out and sometimes merging together into a greater wave of influence. The stone throw is the thing you do—the cause. The ripples it produces are the energy you're sending into your people and your organization—the effect.

> This is the Ripple Effect:
> the cascading impact
> your leadership has
> on the people and
> systems of your organization.

To explore this more deeply, let's look at how the Ripple Effect starts with you and skips to others, to your organization, and beyond.

First, lead yourself—prepare to make a positive impact

Let's begin with a simple statement.

*As a leader, your actions
affect other people and your organization.*

Pretty basic and understandable, so let's expand it a bit.

*As a leader, your actions,
starting with your own state of being,
affect other people and your organization.*

If you've served as a leader or experienced working with a leader, you know this is true. When the leader shows up with his or her strengths, values, and actions all aligned, you can feel it. Leaders who understand how to master leading themselves are more powerful and influential than those who don't.

As a leader, your state of being and doing influences many different layers of your organization: personal, interpersonal, and organizational.

For example, imagine suddenly discovering your health is compromised and that to avoid further damage you must change the way you take care of yourself. The energy, focus, and time it will take to repair your health might, at first glance, seem to take away from your people and organization. Yet without this investment, sooner or later you would be unable to be of service to others.

Or imagine you find yourself needing to have a challenging discussion with an employee who's off track. Avoiding the situation may feel like you're conserving your own time and emotional energy, yet without your action, the situation will just get worse.

Proactive attention to how you as a leader are showing up and taking action can enable you to make bigger, more positive impacts with others.

Second, lead others—influence each person in a genuinely positive way

Let's modify our previous statement:

As a leader, your actions, starting with your own state of being, affect how other people work on an individual level and your organization.

This isn't about you the leader versus a sea of followers. When the leader, already powerfully aligned with himself or herself, respects and builds an enabling relationship with each follower on an individual basis, the entire group of followers is enabled to build strong relationships with each other.

This web of relationships makes the difference between having a company where people say:

"I have to go to work today."

...and having a company where people say:

"I get to go to work today!"

As a leader, how you manage and present yourself dramatically impacts your followers, and the way you connect with each of them dramatically impacts every person in the organization.

For example, imagine getting passionate about a new direction you believe your organization needs to pursue. To some, your passion will come across as exciting and empowering. To others, it may seem dictatorial and oppressive, or even distracting and needless. While you can't control how your passion is received, understanding how each person might react or respond to how you are showing up will enable you to build stronger relationships with each person in your business, thereby helping you achieve better results together. And this web of relationships is surrounded by resources, policies, and processes—the organization.

Third, lead the organization—influence your systems positively

Organizations function not only through relationships but also through structural components like habits, practices, resources, measurements, rules, and processes. Ideally, these structures are designed in harmony for both effectiveness (getting the right things done) and efficiency (get things done right) to get the best results possible in both the short and long term.

While the influence you exert on people will cause them to do things differently within the structure, the influence you exert directly on the organizational layer changes the support structure itself and thereby affects everyone in the organization.

So now our statement expands further still:

> As a leader, your actions,
> starting with your own state of being,
> affect how other people work on an individual level,
> and the systems in which they operate.

For example, imagine finding out that a longstanding policy requiring two signatures for every purchase request is now causing unacceptable delays in your organization. First, you check how the policy aligns with your understanding of needed outcomes and shared values. Second, you collaborate with team members to help them figure out what's really happening and empower them to make it better. This approach allows you and the team to change the policy in a meaningful and productive way, rather than the typical "now hear this" proclamation. Everyone benefits from improved results as well as from a more able and resilient organization.

Your initial action starts a chain reaction that causes positive impacts to others and the organization. The benefits of this chain reaction trigger ripples through the entire organization. They add energy and enthusiasm to the people and processes that make the organization successful. This is the Ripple Effect in action. And with enough momentum, people outside the organization benefit as well.

Ultimately—create ripples beyond your organization

As a transformational leader, the ultimate outcome of your work is to create an organization that can have a lasting, positive impact on clients and customers. In turn, those people will work to make a lasting, positive impact on their clients and customers. And the stone keeps skipping...

For example, imagine that you lead a non-profit like Heifer International.® They raise and donate pregnant animals to people in need around the world. The recipient of a gift is then charged to pass the next offspring to another family in need.

Or imagine you lead a for-profit company that refines material used by other companies to make cancer-fighting drugs. Your company's output is critical to saving people's lives.

In these pay-it-forward examples, it's easy to see how each action you take as leader—your skipping stone—goes from you to others in your organization, to the organization itself, to others creating their own product or service, and to the people who benefit from that product or service. This Ripple Effect continues indefinitely so long as well-intentioned leaders continue to skip stones for positive impact.

It's up to you. How far will your stones travel? What ripples will be created? Will your company be used as a "best practice" for your industry?

While you cannot predict the future, you can influence it. With the right stones and right leadership mindset, you can create amazing ripples that travel quite far indeed.

Start with yourself

Based on my experience working with company leaders, I've discovered that most people find focusing on areas of improvement within the organization and other people easier than beginning with themselves.

"Why focus on me?" they say. "My job is to make a difference out there!" And in some ways, they are completely right.

Yet other leaders instead choose to improve their leadership influence from the inside out. These leaders believe equipping themselves first builds a foundation upon which all their leadership capabilities and results rest.

*In case you feel pressured for results NOW:

Hey, I understand. You don't have time for comprehensive work. You need to improve things immediately. This four-step process is for you:

1. After you finish reading this section, go straight to the **BUT I NEED HELP NOW** section (p. 237) with the symptoms of your most pressing problems.

2. Skim through the list of presenting symptoms and select the section(s) that seem most applicable. Read through and understand the principles and practices to see if they can help resolve your problems.

3. Use one or more exercises under each practice to start moving in the right direction.

4. Once you get some positive feedback, come back and read the rest of the book to ensure you can see how the different pieces of the Ripple model fit together and reinforce one another.

"When I make changes in here," they say, pointing to themselves, "I see corresponding changes out there...", with a sweeping gesture taking in the whole organization.

The truth is that since continuous improvement opportunities exist everywhere within an organization, starting anywhere you can to make a positive impact is as good a place to begin as any.

That said, I believe your best, most lasting results will come from choosing the road less traveled—working first from the inside out.

So here's the four-step process I recommend you follow:*

1. **Work through the book from start to finish.** Start with improving yourself, then move on to improving your relationships, and then work on improving the organization as a whole.

2. **Engage with each principle and practice.** Take notes, mark up the book, and highlight what stands out for you, and work through each practice by completing one or more of the provided exercises.

3. **Build your improvement plan.** Get the free workbook at rippleleader.com and use it to create an action plan focused on making the biggest impact with the least amount of effort as quickly as possible.

4. **Implement your plan.** Increase the positive impact of your leadership on yourself, others, and the organization. Seek support if you need it.

Based on my own personal development and the experience of my clients, starting with yourself will actually generate the best results in the shortest amount of time. While this may sound counterintuitive, it works because strengthening your own core capabilities enables you to more quickly and thoroughly help others, which in turn helps everyone improve the organization.

There's no time like the present

Regardless of which path you take, your success as a Ripple Leader depends on your ability to choose, apply, and adjust the application of the ideas in this book.

If you've ever worked toward any significant, lasting result—like making a successful marriage, building a house, or creating a business, you know you're never really done. Keep that in mind as you work on your own leadership capabilities. The Ripple Effect is about creating an environment where you and everyone else have the best chance for success.

If you want to get the most out of this book, I recommend you visit rippleleader.com and download a free workbook that includes all the exercises and self-assessments, and a framework to create your own action plan to apply the book to your unique situation.

Additionally you may want to create your own improvement journal:

- Get a bound notebook or binder and some Post-It™ flags of different colors. Use the flags to reserve two 10- to 20-page sections each for yourself and for the business, two to three pages for each significant person in your business, and two to three pages for each major client or customer.

- Capture your thoughts in real-time as you read through the book. When you have an insight that relates to you, write it in your section. When you see something that relates to a specific person or client—what you should do differently or perhaps a strength you now realize they have, write it in their section.

- Use the rest of your notebook as workspace to do the exercises from this book you find interesting, then copy your best insights back to the appropriate sections of the notebook. Keep in mind most of the exercises in each section are designed to be completed in 15 minutes or less as a way to practice the concepts and build your positive momentum.

- Finally, when you create an action plan, write the major steps into either your own section or the business section. Voilà! By capturing your own high-level thinking, you have both a valuable reference and a clearer picture of what you're dealing with.

Ready? Let's get started.

SET UP TO CREATE RIPPLES

BY LEADING YOURSELF

In leadership, you can make the biggest impact by first working on yourself.

Everyone is a leader in some way. We provide leadership-by-example to others in everything we do.

When my eldest daughter was four years old, we were playing a game together and having a lot of fun. Once we finished, she turned to me and said, "Dad, when I have kids I'm going to do this with them!"

"Great idea. I really like this game, too!" I replied with a smile.

"No, Dad. I don't mean the game—I mean the way that you're playing with me. I'm going to do things the same way with my kids," Sara replied seriously.

Talk about the pressure of being in a leadership position! There's nothing like being put in your place by a four-year-old.

Whether you have more experience than other team members at something, are in a formal position of authority, or have a perspective that is valuable to a team, I believe you are in a leadership role.

From a leadership role, you have a significant amount of influence over others. You can direct and threaten. You can coerce and reward. You can enable and inspire. And yet, despite all this influence over others, the person you have the most direct influence over is you.

This personal influence is what I mean by Leading Yourself.

There is something in every one of you that waits and listens for the sound of the genuine in yourself. It is the only true guide you will ever have. And if you cannot hear it, you will all of your life spend your days on the ends of strings that somebody else pulls.

Howard Thurman

In Leading Yourself, two principles stand out as key and important:

Principle 1—Leaders' effectiveness is proportional to how well they know themselves. Your foundation is your own values, your desired future, and your capabilities.

Principle 2—Leaders are judged more by what they don't than by what they do. Talk is cheap. Action is priceless. You have to be in action on what's important, persevere, and renew yourself.

Leading Yourself is first because how you align yourself and get yourself into action is the way you can positively influence others and the organization. Great results become more possible as you become more consciously familiar with the importance of being before doing.

On *being* versus *doing*

My grandfather taught me a lot about life. One of the most important lessons was the downside of judging your own worth strictly on what you can do rather than on how you are being. For most of his life, he was able to do amazing things like build cabins, train horses, and create a loving family. He became bitter and angry, however, when emphysema caught up with him in his late 70s, tethering him to a supplemental oxygen canister.

Held back by breathlessness, my grandfather grew to feel worthless because he wasn't able to do what he once could. Consequently, he took out that disappointment and anger on those around him during the last years of his life.

My grandfather's transformation was strongly influenced by our do-oriented culture. Look no further than networking events to see this in action. "So, what do you do?" is almost always the first question people ask each other. Why this emphasis on doing? Because accomplishments are valued much more than simply being, at least by most people. Wise people through the ages, however, recognized that the quality of one's being is often more important than raw ability or the accomplishment of tasks. Our being must come first because it informs and improves our abilities, thereby allowing us to achieve accomplishments that truly matter.

Principle 1
Leaders' effectiveness is proportional to how well they know themselves

Principle 2
Leaders are judged more by what they don't than by what they do

Principle 3
People discover their best selves through being respected by a leader

Principle 4
People multiply a leader's power only as much as that power is shared

Principle 5
Organizations are designed to get the results they are getting

Principle 6
Organizations generating waste are generating opportunities for improvement

Deep self-understanding is the foundation for a leader's potential impact.

Principle 1

Leaders' effectiveness is proportional to how well they know themselves

You know it when a leader who knows who she is and where she's going walks into the room. You feel her confidence electrify the group. You sense the room's momentum shift in her direction. And you know you can believe what you see and hear. This experience is possible because it's easy to understand where the leader is coming from. Values and direction are consistent, vivid, and inclusive. Language is welcoming and easy to relate to. Everything is connected; nothing is wasted. Without such alignment, a leader's direction is fuzzy and character is uncertain. When a leader lacks alignment, she is quick to lose followers.

The challenge is to look in the mirror and push ourselves to have the same clarity about ourselves we see in others who are highly aligned. It's easier not to do the exploratory surgery or the exercise program or the new diet because we don't have to see how we're contributing to our own challenges. We don't want to be responsible for following through on the rehab or getting up early in the morning or not eating carbs because that's hard work. Denial is the drug of choice for most people—and that's exactly why knowing yourself and the impact you want to make with your life can be such a springboard to exceptional leadership.

Why smart leaders start with personal alignment

For decades, Kouzes and Posner, the authors of *The Leadership Challenge*[1] have studied hundreds of thousands of leaders across countries, cultures, organization structures, genders, education, and age groups. From their massive data sets filled with variables, a consistent pattern for effective leadership emerged. In the researchers' own words, "For people to follow someone willingly, the majority of constituents believe the leader must be honest, forward-looking, inspiring, and competent."

Two of the four qualities—honest and competent—can be summed up in one word: credibility. A leader with these qualities is believable and trustworthy.

The remaining two qualities—forward-looking and inspiring—distinguish Ripple Leaders from their unremarkable peers. They see ahead into the future and guide others toward it. This visionary quality is powerful. Yet, without the foundation of credibility, even the best vision will not help. As Kouzes and Posner say in their First Law of Leadership:

> If you don't believe in the messenger,
> you won't believe the message.

In their Second Law of Leadership, Kouzes and Posner define the best way to build credibility:

> DWYSYWD: Do What You Say You Will Do.

To me, having my words, thoughts, and deeds all in alignment establishes leadership credibility. I do my best to say only what I can do, and to do all I say. Over time, I found that this commitment to myself enabled others to find me credible in the workplace. But even though I was helping teams perform very well, I had a nagging feeling something was missing.

Eventually I discovered that truly great leaders go beyond credibility and seek alignment among higher values, their personal vision, and their capabilities.

Ripple Leadership requires such alignment because without applied understanding of our own strengths and weaknesses—which are both opportunities and limitations—we are likely to end up using a tremendous amount of energy trying to be someone we are not.

I have fallen into this trap myself. In fact, I can recall every time someone has helped me understand my limitations as a leader. While these reality checks were awkward and even painful in the moment, by listening to people who had the courage to let me know where I was coming up short, I was able to better understand and apply my capabilities. Of course, this usually happened when those limitations were completely obvious to everyone but me—sort of like when you walk past a mirror after you gave a great presentation only to discover there was spinach stuck between your front teeth!

However, if we as leaders apply our strengths disconnected from higher values focused on honoring people, we are at risk of transforming ourselves into dictators and megalomaniacs. Sadly, history continues to record people around the world in leadership positions using power and wealth against other people.

So my definition of powerful alignment for Ripple Leaders involves three major components: values, vision, and personal capability.

Get into alignment

To help you leverage this principle in your own leadership, I've selected the three most powerful practices that have helped my clients get into personal self-alignment. Each practice has its own section, complete with short exercises to get you thinking and immediately engaging with the practice.

1. *Decide what matters most.* Your personal values are the best compass for your unique journey.

2. *Chart your own course.* Picturing your own personal future helps you see what steps to take—or not—to get there.

3. *Know where you're awesome.* People often don't recognize their own strengths—and you cannot tap what you do not know.

Each of these practices is critical to building the leadership foundation you need to positively affect your team and organization. If you are to be successful with the principles and practices that follow, you first must master yourself.

Ripple leadership starts with you and how you hold and launch each stone.

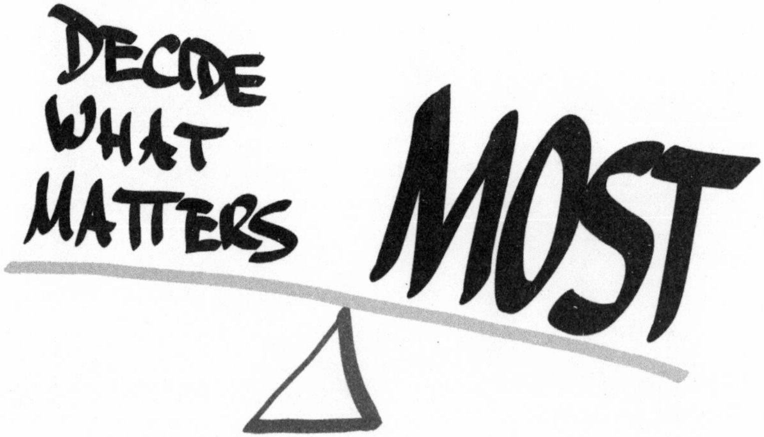
DECIDE
WHAT
MATTERS
MOST

Practice 1.1 | **Decide what matters most**

Your personal values are the best compass for your unique journey.

A leader's personal belief system is defined by his or her values and informs how he or she perceives and interacts with the world. Further, when we consciously know our own values, we are able to better understand the values held by others. We are able to be more aware of the biases our own values bring to a situation, for good or for ill. We also become more empathetic when we are more self-aware.

Without self-awareness, many leaders tacitly live out their values and unknowingly define other people's values purely in relation to their own. I find that people in leadership positions who aren't aware of their own values have a greater tendency to fall into the "you're with me or you're against me" attitude about others. By not consciously and explicitly understanding what matters to them and why, these leaders often feel the need to defend themselves, and by doing so miss the opportunity to appreciate the richness and usefulness of people who may have different values.

In contrast, leaders who consciously know what matters most to them can be more objective in seeking ways to live out their values fully, while helping others do the same.

For example, one of my core values is abundance. I believe abundance enables people to rise above greed and scarcity to bring out the best in themselves and others. Scarcity thinking says there isn't enough for everyone, so you must get what you need without regard to others. Abundance is more about empathy, inquiry, and significance—opening up new possibilities that embrace your full self and seeking opportunities to

This practice is helpful if:

- You find people guessing what you want, and they're often wrong.

- Employees are forming "us versus them" camps and taking things more personally than is helpful.

- The organization is underperforming to your expectations.

fully engage others. It's about helping create value first and then receiving value yourself as a byproduct of what you co-created.

In some industries, scarcity rules. Your win is my loss, so I'm going to do whatever it takes to make you lose. Labor versus management, lawyer versus lawyer, your sports team versus mine.

Some people in leadership positions choose to win over their customers, colleagues, or employees in the short term by extracting all the value they can, and lose long term in the process by alienating anyone from wanting to work with them.

On the other hand, you can be like Seth Godin and lead with generosity.

The power [in gift-giving] lies in the
creation of abundance. A trade leaves things
as they were, with no external surplus.
A gift always creates a surplus as it spreads.

— Seth Godin

In his book *Linchpin*, Seth advocates for people to be generous givers as a way for them to create more value for the organization and themselves. Allow me to share how Seth walks his talk.

In promoting *Linchpin*, Seth gave out advance copies to people who donated to the Acumen Fund, an organization committed to helping people build sustainable businesses solving social, economic, and environmental problems around the world. I happened to be one of those people who "bought" the book this way.

Included in the book was a simple sheet of paper telling me what Seth thought was the most important part of the book—and a request to share my thoughts about the book online. Little did I know that Seth had only sent out advance copies to people like me and was not using established methods and professional reviewers to promote the book. I wrote and posted an honest and heartfelt review, which was well-ranked by other readers. Seth chose to give me a small link in one of his blog postings, and our company still sees more people visiting our website today as a result. By encouraging me to be generous, and by being generous himself, Seth has cemented in my mind the potential of being a generous gift giver.

Oh, and then he sent me (and the other donors) another copy of the book with a request to pass it on. That's knowing and living out your values.

This following exercise is a favorite of facilitators, trainers, and leadership authors. Getting more clear about your values is one of the most important steps to fully living them.

The value we receive is a byproduct of the value we help create.

This exercise is meant to help you scratch the surface of understanding what you hold most dear and get some sense of why you do the things you do. Use the table of values at right to complete the following activities. The blank areas are for you to write in values that you don't see on the table.

1. **Determine your top 10 values.** First, cross out all values that don't make your top 10.

2. **Reduce the list to your top 3 values.** Next, underline those top 3.

3. **Reduce the top 3 to the top most value for you.** (Yes, it's hard.) Box in your number one value.

4. **Dig down to get more insight into what's most important for you.** Once you've identified your values, think about how they show up in your work and home life, and write them down in your notebook. To take this further, spend another few minutes and write out what your top values mean in your own terms and using real-life examples or stories that demonstrate them.

Refer to this over time and refine as needed to give yourself the best chance of harnessing your values to get where you most want to end up.

Abundance	Growth	Service
Achievement	Happiness	Simplicity
Autonomy	Harmony	Spirituality
Beauty	Health	Strength
Challenge	Hope	Teamwork
Communication	Humor	Transparency
Competence	Independence	Trust
Competition	Innovation	Truth
Creativity	Integrity	Variety
Curiosity	Intelligence	Wisdom
Decisiveness	Joy	
Dependability	Kindness	
Discipline	Love	
Diversity	Loyalty	
Effectiveness	Open-mindedness	
Efficiency	Patience	
Empathy	Power	
Equality	Productivity	
Family	Prosperity	
Flexibility	Quality	
Fun	Recognition	
Friendship	Respect	
Freedom	Risk Taking	
Generosity	Security	

CHART YOUR OWN COURSE

Practice 1.2 | **Chart your own course**

Picturing your own personal future helps you see what steps to take—or not—to get there.

It's said that without vision, the people perish.[2] But what about the leader without vision? He perishes just the same yet in a far more subtle way. I don't think that's a future you care to experience. So to steer clear of a slow demise, take the time and energy to clarify your vision for yourself and for those who look up to you.

The clarity of the end goal increases the clarity of actions needed to achieve it.

My idea of a successful vision is a picture, painted with words, that provides clarity to every decision you make. It is a tall tower that is very far away and has a blinking light on it—a beacon to guide your every step as you head toward it. It is such a compelling image that it is burned into your retinas, so that in the darkest of times you can close your eyes and still see which way to go next.

How does your vision ultimately end up?

Some leaders develop this clarity by, as Stephen Covey said, "Beginning with the end in mind."[3] I often apply this approach with my clients, as I did several years ago when I led a group of construction business owners through a guided visualization. After having the group close their eyes and imagine moving forward three years into the future, to their own memorial service, I asked a series of questions:

This practice is helpful if:

- You are constantly opportunistic and nothing lasts long before the next better opportunity comes along.

- Employees complain they are constantly subjected to the "flavor of the month," and you don't see people committing to change.

- The organization is splintered with functions working toward different goals.

- Who is there at your service? Who from your family, your work, your community?
- What do you want those people to say about you?
- What is the mood in the room? How are people interacting?
- What would you want people to carry on as your legacy?

Afterward, I asked people to write down their thoughts. A few minutes later I noticed a burly landscape contractor was visibly shaken. Checking in, I asked if he would share his thoughts with the group.

"I have to change what I'm doing—today!" he blurted out. "Or in three years there's no way the people I care about would say what I want them to say!"

That's clarity.

Once you imagine a picture of your desired future, keep in mind it is merely a snapshot of tomorrow through today's lens. Tomorrow's lens is likely to be a bit different. You experience a crisis. A loved one becomes ill or despondent. Your organization suffers a setback. You win the lottery. Life continues to throw us challenges that shape and test what we want now and into the future.

The following exercise gives you another way to picture your desired future. To use it or any other visioning exercise, you will get the best result if you imagine yourself creating frames for your own personal stop-motion animation. That's where one picture leads to another slightly different picture and another and another. When you do this with visioning, you end up with a succession of pictures that, flipped through at the right speed, blend into a seamless movie of your life as you want it to unfold in front of you.

As director of your own personal movie, you may not get to pick the exact right camera angle or background light and how it ends, yet you do get to choose your perspective, the meaning you discern from being part of it, and how you would like it to end. It's really up to you.

Ready to roll?

What do you want people to say about your after you're gone?

Exercise 1.2a | **Picturing the future you most want**

This simple method will enable you to begin extracting the elements of your own personal vision. The best part about this exercise—which I call Picturing the Future—is that it intentionally creates a very rough-hewn vision. Instead of a wordsmithed-to-death, ready-to-chisel-in-granite proclamation, this is a roughed-out, simple set of criteria of what you want and don't want to help guide you on your journey.

1. **To start Picturing the Future, get three blank pieces of paper and a pen.** Write Achieve on the top of one sheet, Avoid on the next, and Preserve on the last.

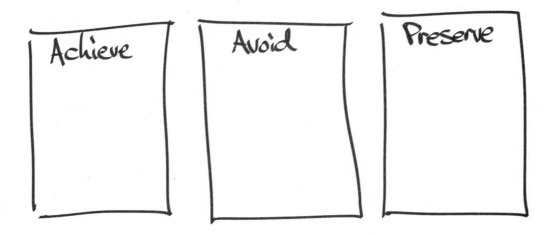

2. **Imagine yourself five years in the future.** Everything is just how you want it. Ask yourself the following questions to clearly describe your desired future:

   - What have you achieved that you most wanted?

   - What have you avoided that you didn't want?

   - What have you preserved that you wanted to keep?

3. **Write down at least five items for each category.** More is better. Notice that the questions are not a function of *HOW*. You want to get as close as possible to the end result of what you aspire to achieve. This approach grants you the most freedom and flexibility in the methods you might choose to pursue those goals.

4. **Review your list for must-haves and nice-to-haves.** Mark the must-haves.

5. **Use the list to guide your decision-making going forward.** Transfer the finalized list into your notebook. When you need to make a significant decision, look at your list. Ask yourself how your available options help you achieve, avoid, and preserve what you have identified as most important to you. Choose the option that maximizes your success criteria and doesn't violate any of them, then proceed with confidence because that option is on the path to your desired future. If you don't have an option that works, see if you can change the conditions around the least-worst choice so that it fits with your success criteria. If you can't make it work, just say no. It's not on your path.

Refine your achieve-avoid-preserve criteria as you use them to help yourself stay in alignment. If you have a choice that passes the filter yet you feel is still wrong, add the criteria that would screen it out. Likewise, if you have a choice that feels right yet doesn't pass, tweak your criteria set to enable it (and other opportunities like it) to be implemented. I encourage you to revisit this exercise at least annually to add further sharpness to your picture of your best personal future.

As you use tools like Picturing the Future, you will begin to more clearly discern your life's purpose: why you are here.

Navigating by your energy level can help you find your purpose

I have not always known my life's purpose. In fact, it took several years after I left my parents' home before my purpose caught up with me. Once it did, I was confident in my direction and the impacts I would make along the way. My biggest wish for my children is that they understand their own purpose as early in their own lives as possible.

I believe that passion—the interest that drives you deep into something—is one of the best tools to discern your life's purpose. Passion is like an energy source that emanates from your purpose. If you are willing to pay attention to and align with it, it can guide you in, just like a navigational system.

When I was learning to fly, I discovered a radio navigational instrument that senses and displays the strength of a signal sent on selected frequencies by special transmitters located around the country. To use the device, the pilot plots a destination through all the known points between origin and destination, then figures out the angle of approach for each waypoint. To make sure the plane is flying precisely toward the waypoint, all the pilot has to do is dial in the frequency of that approach and then watch the signal strength on the gauge. Once the needle rises, the pilot turns the plane to keep the signal strong and as a result flies right toward the intended destination.

Passion is just like that signal-strength meter. Once you have an idea of what interests you and where you want to go, simply move forward until you feel your passion rise, then continue to adjust your course so that your passion keeps coming on strong. And this passion isn't the flash-in-the-pan type that comes from indulging your appetites. No, it's the deep, gut-level passion you feel when you are doing your best work and using your natural and developed strengths. Navigating in this manner will keep you oriented toward your life's purpose.

As you are paying attention to your energy levels, beware of fear. It can masquerade as passion and pull you off track. Here's how you can tell the difference:

> Fear can be a great motivator, yet it provides no lasting direction.

To illustrate, let's say you and I are sitting together, talking, when flames suddenly burst out in one corner of the room. The shocking sight of the flames, the blast of heat on our faces, and the sharp smell of smoke would instantly motivate us to do something—NOW! We would be faced with an instantaneous choice: fight the fire, or get out?

Far too many people, in real life and in business, unconsciously choose to fight what they are afraid of rather than consciously choose to turn the opposite direction and instead seek opportunities for greater success. And far too many people end up burned as a result.

A reality I've seen from my work with clients over the years is:

> You get what you focus on.

If you focus on what's "bad" and try not to do that, at best you'll end up with "not bad." If instead you focus on what you want, I believe you have a significantly better chance to achieve what you want. Use fear and what you don't want only to help you discern and turn toward what you do want. Consciously figuring out your purpose can be liberating because it both clarifies your perspective and reinforces the importance of how you believe things should be.

Exercise 1.2b | **Discern your purpose**

Lance Secretan has written 14 books on inspirational leadership and often speaks on helping people discern their purpose.[4] He asks his readers Big Questions like, "Why are you here? What reality are you here to make happen?" While related to the Picturing the Future exercise you just did, this exercise goes further by looking at a larger, more universal picture and timeline out as far as you can imagine:

1. **Figure out what riles you up**. Get out your notebook and take just a few minutes to write down whatever you see in the world that really ticks you off, personally and professionally. This is your time for a personal gripe session, so let loose! Those pet peeves are clues to the kind of reality you are here to help create. Pick your top-most irritants and put a star next to each one.

2. **Pivot to the opposite.** Now take a few more minutes to imagine the opposite: You are in a distant future where all those starred conditions no longer exist because they are replaced with their complete opposites. (This is sometimes known as the "magic-wand" state, as if you had a magic wand and could wave it to get whatever you truly wanted.) While you've got those positive states in your mind, write down how you want things to be with as much detail as you can. Don't hold back! If you get stuck, look back to the previous exercise around your most important values. There should be some strong clues about what you want for the universe.

3. **The difference between these two states is your purpose for being.** Without getting too metaphysical, let's say you're here to help the universe move from what's wrong with it to what's most needed. So take a few more minutes and write down what you see as the "delta," or difference, between what you don't want and what you do want.

While this is just the tip of the iceberg, this brief exercise is meant to provide you with some clarification or validation of what you are working toward personally and professionally. Of course, now that you have more clarity, you also have a corresponding responsibility to make your positive future a reality. I believe this is what Gandhi meant when he said, "Be the change you want to see in the world."[5] Making sure you are striving for a positive purpose will make your Ripple Leadership all the more powerful—and help your ripples reach far and wide.

Your purpose should bring out the very best in you: your deepest strengths, your greatest talents, your highest values.

After having a clear personal picture and connection to your personal passions, it's critical to understand your strengths to be able to use them to effectively lead yourself.

Practice 1.3 | **Know where you're awesome**

People often don't recognize their own strengths. And you cannot tap what you do not know.

We've all heard stories in which an otherwise unremarkable person demonstrates that she or he has an amazing untapped capability. Sometimes this ability is revealed during a crisis, when someone steps forward to help in a moment of great need. Examples abound: Winston Churchill defying the Nazis in World War II. Mahatma Gandhi liberating the people of India. A mother singlehandedly lifting a car off her trapped child.

These people must have had some sense of their own capability to even attempt feats like these, and it's possible some of their abilities were dormant and awakened by the imminent need.

As leaders, we need to know our capability before the need arises. When we understand our strengths and weaknesses, we know our potential contribution better, and how and where we could use help from others. And we understand how not to overdo our strengths.

How to define "strengths"?

Marcus Buckingham is a strengths evangelist.[6] He helped create a movement that instructs people on how to understand and apply their innate strengths in their careers. The statistic he frequently quotes is that less than 20 percent of people feel they are applying their strengths at work. He has pledged his life to moving that statistic upward, helping people appreciate their strengths so we all can use them more.

A few years ago at a presentation, I asked Marcus a question: "Is a strength something you do well or is it something you love doing?" He shared that

This practice
is helpful if:

- You are surprised / disappointed other people can't do the things you can.

- Employees question their own abilities, and prejudge others' abilities.

- The organization is slow to respond to where you think it should be.

he sees a strength as something you're excited to do and you feel stronger doing. In essence, his answer to my question was "Yes."

Interestingly, in my work I find that many leaders don't recognize—and even discredit—their own strengths. This happens when people unthinkingly see the abilities that come easily to them as not important or valuable. In most cases, people are simply unaware that what they are doing is exceptional.

For example, when I pointed out to one of my clients how she positively helped in a very challenging situation involving her direct report, the response I got was, "No big deal. It was easy. Anyone in that situation would do what I did, right?"

"Actually, no," I replied. "They wouldn't because they can't." In answer to her somewhat puzzled look, I continued. "They can't see the potential buried deep within others. They can't help people correct themselves without making the other person feel stupid or wrong. They can't think of creative yet practical ideas on the fly. The things you do without flexing a muscle are hard if not impossible for others to do. You do these things extraordinarily well, and if you enjoy doing them and feel strong while doing them, you need to know they are your strengths."

Knowing your unique strengths as a leader enables you to apply yourself effectively in the situations where you can have the most influence. Rather than trying to be all things to all people—a common and unobtainable desire of people in leadership positions—you can consciously choose how to use your strengths to make a difference in a specific way. This enables you to choose skipping stones that work well for you so you can create ripples that optimize your own personal strengths.

Yet there's an insidious challenge that stands in the way of keeping our strengths as strengths. My mentor, Richard Reardon, shared some wisdom with me around this early on in our work together:

Any strength, overdone or used without thought, can become a weakness.

That is, when a strength is applied to excess, a corresponding weakness often emerges. This weakness can create negative effects that are as detrimental to the overall desired result as if the strength wasn't present to begin with.

More is not always better—a different view of strengths and weaknesses

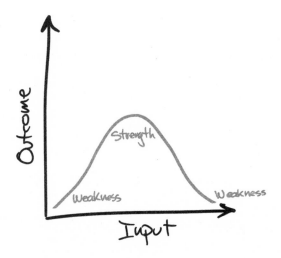

Here's a simple graph representing the typical relationship between inputs and outcome.

Along the bottom, we have the amount of input, starting at nothing on the left and increasing toward the right. Along the left side, we have the amount of result, or outcome, again starting at nothing on the bottom and increasing as we go up. The curve on the diagram represents the results we get from the input we provide.

This diagram is universally applicable to nearly any desired outcome and input combination relating to natural systems. For example: effectiveness of work as an outcome of the amount of time spent at work; effectiveness of a relationship as an outcome of how much communication is occurring; or even overall health as an outcome of the number of calories consumed.

In this model, both low and high inputs are ineffective. Somewhere in between too much and too little is the just-right, Goldilocks sweet spot. We tend to label a person as having a "weakness" if they are in those areas where the results are poor (too little or too much) and having a "strength" if they are working where the results are good (the top of the curve).

More is always better, right?

Unfortunately, many individuals—including leaders—fall victim to the "more is always better" trap. The trap is very easy to fall into because, until you reach the top of the curve, more inputs absolutely DO produce better results! We provide a little more input, get slightly better results, do more, get even better results, and so on. This success lulls people into believing their growth trajectory can go on forever. That is, until you hit the top of the curve—the infamous "point of diminishing returns," where the more you do, the worse results you get.

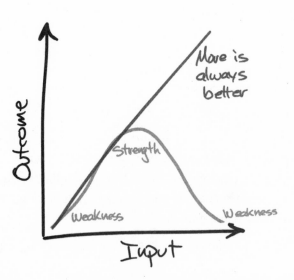

Goldilocks curve

Counter-intuitive results

I must admit that when we first start working with a new client, whether an executive team or a single leader, they are often to the right of where the "more is always better" line has diverged from the "this is what's really happening" curve. They aren't getting what they need, yet they don't know anything else to do except more of what worked in the past, and as a result are getting worse and worse outcomes. Sometimes they are in a fair amount of denial. They truly believe that the more they do, the better the results they will get, and they have trouble accepting that reality is actually far below their expectations. The good news is that we're usually able to help them essentially ease off on the accelerator and immediately get better results.

However, most hard-driving leaders find this advice completely counterintuitive: "Chris, you're telling me if I do less of this I'll get better results? That just flies in the face of all my experience up to now!" Exactly. So we ease off a little on the control of details, or need for involvement in decisions, or asking Inquisition-style questions—and as a result we get more of what we want and an environment where everyone can feel more successful and not trapped by the leader's strengths gone bad.

The way to stay out of this thinking trap in the first place is to determine and closely monitor the results you desire (Outcome) as you apply effort (Input). When you begin to notice a decline in the return on your investment, you're likely cresting the top of the results curve.

Physical fitness performance tracking is a great example of this paradigm in action. At the beginning of each year, many people make a resolution to go to the gym every day. These same people don't realize that going to the gym is actually an input and not the desired outcome (e.g., stronger muscles, improved body composition, etc.). Consequently, they huff and they puff and they overdo it. Overtraining, burnout, and poor recovery typically lead to subconscious avoidance of the gym, which decays into abandoning getting fit, at least until next year. The problem here is confusing the outcome you need with the input you can measure—and not paying attention to creating an input you can sustain.

On the other hand, if you instead choose a goal like "I will fit comfortably into my favorite pants," you can more easily see the results you are achieving, empowering you to adjust your inputs of eating and exercise as your results begin to change from the same amount of input. When you achieve this goal you can decide to stabilize or take on another, such as "I want to compete in the Ironman Triathlon." As long as you are measuring the results you get compared to what you are willing to put in, you will be setting yourself up for success.

More is not always better. Better is better.

Marshall Goldsmith wrote an entire book, *What Got You Here Won't Get You There*,[7] advising executives on the 21 bad habits they should do less of to get better results. His counterintuitive yet time-tested advice lines up perfectly with our Goldilocks curve model. This wisdom is the essence of preventing strengths from becoming weaknesses.

As an example: A few years ago we were working with a brilliant and driven CEO from a technology startup company. One of his strengths-gone-bad was Adding Too Much Value (from Goldsmith's bad habits). Whenever senior executives would bring a project to improve the product offering or the company itself, the CEO would ask question after question, piggybacking his own ideas and refinements onto the original project until the executive would, as one person told us, "crawl out of the room, beaten and bloody." What this CEO did not realize was that his well-intentioned, innovative thinking was doing the exact opposite of his intent. It was causing people to feel ineffective and unworthy, and was actually driving innovative thinking down and out of the company. Once the feedback did get to the CEO, he was stunned. "My goal has always been to show keen interest and support innovation. I help by asking questions that improve our results." Up to that point, he had no idea that his approach wasn't helping and was actually seen as an interrogation no one wanted to go through.

To manage and grow our strengths, we need to be more aware of the point of diminishing returns and adjust our inputs to stay in our own personal sweet spot. Since it can be challenging for people to approach you with what might be taken as bad news, one of the best ways to raise your awareness is through self-administered assessments.

Seeing yourself in a mirrored disco ball

Personality assessments can be extremely helpful, if used in the right way. I often share with clients that assessments are like a mirrored disco ball, rotating slowly in the middle of the ceiling. When you look at the ball, every so often in one mirrored tile you get a very clear glimpse of one part of yourself from a perspective you don't normally have. That little mirrored picture is not you nor does it define you, and by definition it cannot be comprehensive. Yet the more glimpses you get of yourself, the fewer your blind spots and the more understanding you have of who you really are. As I see it, the power of assessments rests in improved understanding of yourself so that you can apply your strengths in ways that benefit you, others, and the organization.

Because assessments can be used to label people rather than reveal strengths, I work to make sure people have a chance to review and interpret their own personal results and get to choose what they think is most accurate and what they want to share with their team. While labeling someone an ENTP or a High D or a type Number 7 may feel like a valuable shortcut, I believe it can result in a person getting stuck in a box that limits his or her ability to contribute fully.

Most assessments measure preferences, and even then should not be taken as absolute. Disco balls aren't a good way to understand the crowd on the dance floor.

Here is a short list of a few assessments you can use to improve self-understanding:

- **DISC**—This assessment creates a behavior profile that provides insight into your natural approach to work in four areas:

  - How you respond to problems and challenges.

  - How you influence others to your point of view.

  - How you respond to the pace of the environment.

  - How you respond to rules and procedures set by others.

  There are many versions of the DISC available. Some reports are better than others at helping you bring out your strengths.

- **Workplace Motivators**—This tool provides information about the inner drives, or "whys" underlying your behavior and ways to better engage, motivate, and reward yourself in accordance with your personal motivators.

- **Thomas-Kilman Conflict Inventory**—This assessment indicates your preferences in dealing with conflict, primarily how much you focus on your needs and the needs of the other person(s) you're experiencing conflict with.

- **Leadership Practices Inventory**—This tool measures the frequency of leadership behaviors using both self-awareness and anonymous feedback from those around you to enable you to make behavioral changes and improve your leadership effectiveness.

- **Strengths Finder**—This assessment indicates your top naturally recurring patterns of thought, feeling, or behavior to enable you to understand and apply your strengths more effectively.

There are many other instruments, such as Myers-Briggs Type Indicator and Enneagram. Assessments like these are valuable as long as they reflect some truth back to you that serves you to better apply your personal strengths.

Exercise 1.3 | **Discover your sweet spot**

This exercise covers some activities you can use to uncover strengths you may not be fully aware of, and reaffirm those strengths you already know you have. Some of the components of this exercise could easily take longer than 15 minutes—and whatever time you invest here will pay significant dividends over the rest of your working career.

1. **Discover strengths that are hidden in plain sight.** Go to a clean sheet of paper in your notebook and brainstorm a list of what you find easy and fun. Circle or add anything other people compliment you on. Look for patterns, then validate them with a trusted source, such as a significant other, to see if you've uncovered new strengths.

2. **Take a third-party strengths assessment.**[8] While it will likely take you longer than 15 minutes to take an assessment and interpret your results, it can be one of the best tools to help you objectively gage your strengths. Ideally you should work with a person who can help you get as much out of the assessment as possible. We've never had a client regret spending time learning about their strengths.

3. **Journal your accomplishments each day for a week.** Take a few minutes each evening to write down what you are most proud of and do really well. Also note what is frustrating and challenging to you. Stay alert for trends that can help you better identify your strengths. Electronic journals can be great—I enjoy the paper-based *10+ Journal*[9] by Ian Matthews.

It's normal to be a little uncomfortable exploring your strengths—many people feel they should know themselves well enough that this should be unnecessary. As I often tell my clients: "In the absence of other information, I believe I'm normal. So if you're just like me you're normal. And if you're not like me you're abnormal." Looking at your strengths from a slightly different perspective than usual can help you see what makes you unique—which in turn enables you to apply them in a deliberate way.

Self-Assessment

How well do you know yourself, your aspirations, and your strengths?

Personal self-understanding is vital to building a strong foundation for your leadership. This simple assessment can help you see how well you understand yourself in relation to the practices we just covered.

The questions below are to help you explore further which practice is most beneficial to start working on. Often the best practice to work on is not the one where there is the most significant difference between where you are and where you want to be. Instead, it is the one that is holding you and your team back from success, showing up again and again as a stumbling block people trip over.

Asking yourself what's holding you back will begin to uncover paths to success that you haven't yet looked at. Writing in your notebook is a highly-effective way to begin moving from thought into action.

Consider these questions...

- Which practice stands out as important and urgent for you to address?
- How will working on it help you, others, and the organization?
- What's holding you back from working on it?

You may not have answers right now—and that's completely ok. Write down in your notebook what you're thinking and where you see yourself right now. As you work through the book, going through the effort of documenting your current state will give you the best chance of finding solutions that work with your personal style of leadership.

Look at each set of statements and mentally mark an X where you are on the continuum of that practice. Think of this more as a baseline than a report card. And don't cheat yourself. Dishonest assessments are not valuable to you.

Where are you right now on the following practices?

Practice 1.1 | **Decide what matters most**

| I have not yet defined my values. | I understand and use my values every day. | Others need to follow my values. |

Practice 1.2 | **Chart your own course**

| I work day-to-day and hope for the best. | My picture of the future pulls me forward toward it every day. | I live on the horizon, sometimes forgetting about today. |

Practice 1.3 | **Know where you're awesome**

| My capabilities are simply whatever I do. | I have validated and apply my strengths, avoiding my weaknesses. | I'm clear that other people need to work around my capabilities. |

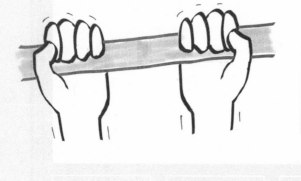

Principle 2

Leaders are judged more by what they don't than by what they do

Principle 1
Leaders' effectiveness is proportional to how well they know themselves

Principle 3
People discover their best selves through being respected by a leader

Principle 4
People multiply a leader's power only as much as that power is shared

Principle 5
Organizations are designed to get the results they are getting

Principle 6
Organizations generating waste are generating opportunities for improvement

Principle 2

Leaders are judged more by what they don't than by what they do

As Will Rogers said, "It's great to be on the right track, but you'll get run over if you just sit there."[10] When you take action as a leader, you make things happen. Yet more importantly, people get to see what you are made of and what you care about. They get to see the example you want them to follow. And if you don't do what's important, they will see that as well.

Facing my own limitations far from home

I was part of a 35-member military team that built a base in Albania to provide reconnaissance over Bosnia-Herzegovina. The mission was to provide pictures of who was where to help enforce peace in the war-torn region. During the initial phase of base building, I was in action as a leader—keeping the plan in front of us, making sure the right equipment and supplies were there, and working through the inevitable issues. With a capable and motivated team, we finished a challenging task a day ahead of schedule.

But when I returned a few months later to take down the base, I found that the team was tired and the path to the goal was much more complicated. I ended up spending most of my time in a tent on a computer planning logistics instead of walking around helping. It wasn't as satisfying for me, and I'm fairly sure the team's perception of my leadership suffered. Why? Because I wasn't in action when I needed to be. No one but me had the authority to tell me to step up to all my

As a leader, no one will force you to do the things that matter — and neither will they forget if you don't.

responsibilities, yet everyone (including me) judged my action and inaction accordingly.

It takes action to skip stones — especially those that are uncomfortable or difficult for you as a leader — in order to make the kinds of ripples you want in others and your organization.

To be in action as a leader, you must follow these three practices in the second principle of being a Ripple Leader:

1. ***Do the hard stuff.*** Doing what's important is the hardest and most rewarding work you will do as a leader.

2. ***Risk and be resilient.*** Leaders deal with the unknown first — and then must adjust to achieve the outcome.

3. ***Charge your own batteries.*** Caring for and strengthening yourself ensures effectiveness that makes your leadership possible.

In essence, these practices are you setting up and throwing the stones: holding each stone carefully, curling your arm back, and then smoothly releasing the stone at just the right angle and velocity to maximize the skips and ripples influencing others, the organization, and beyond. Without your willing engagement in these practices, you aren't a leader. You're just an interested bystander.

This practice is helpful if:

- You are a happy firefighter fueled by and addicted to urgency.

- Employees are complaining of "whiplash" from constant changes of direction.

- Lots of activity is occurring in the organization, yet not much progress is being made.

Practice 2.1 | **Do the hard stuff**

Doing what's most important is the hardest and most rewarding work you will do as a leader.

In his seminal book *The Seven Habits of Highly Effective People*,[11] Stephen R. Covey wrote about being "caught in the thick of thin things." He developed a grid that showed four quadrants of different amounts of urgency and importance. The paradigm is his. The single word summaries in each quadrant are mine.

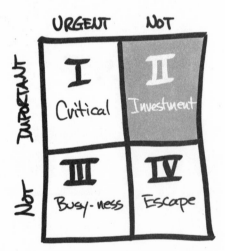

What's Important vs. Urgent based on Covey's model

Activities in the upper-left quadrant are urgent and important. These are fairly easy to see, since if you don't address these issues immediately, very bad things will happen. Fleeing a burning building or dealing with a major client who is threatening to leave are good examples. Most people attack critical items, or those dealing with life and limb, first. From there, they go in order of urgency based on how much time is available and what it will take to resolve it. The challenge here is that it is easy to get confused about which items are Critical, and which are just Busy-ness.

Most people are addicted to Busy-ness: things that call out to be done NOW yet really don't add significant value to our lives. We like to stay in Busy-ness because it feels like we're accomplishing things, and it takes a while to get going on the "hard stuff." Examples abound: checking email, updating Twitter and Facebook, reorganizing your desk drawer. When I find myself doing these activities to the exclusion of Investment activities, I know I am stuck in Busy-ness or Escape and have lost sight of importance.

A leader focused on importance first accomplishes what is Critical, and then makes Investments in his or her long-term success. Unfortunately, these Investments will never be demanded of you, and without conscious effort, you will only discover how important they are when it's too late. These Quadrant II activities are the subtly-important-yet-not-urgent planning, renewal, and relationship-building tasks and goals where we can invest our lives to reap benefits over time. They are easy to put off, yet if we neglect them, we will pay a price long after we decide to do something that feels pressing at the time. To understand the real value of working on what's important, ask anyone who's had a health or relationship failure that was a long time coming.

So as a leader, it is critical to work on Investment activities because the ongoing effectiveness of yourself, others, and the organization depends so heavily on them. Without your own personal health, you cannot help the organization. Without trusting relationships, your team members will turn on each other when they face a crisis. Without a plan, we will all

> A key test to discern importance from urgency is to ask yourself, "If I don't do this, what's the worst thing that will happen three hours, three weeks, or three years from now?" If you can live with the impact, it's simply urgent. If not, it's important.

stumble around trying to figure out what to do. And without a continuous flow of your efforts—your intentional skipping of important stones in the right places—the ripples of your influence and the entire organization's success will dissipate and then disappear.

You're the only person who can choose to do powerful activities like building trust in others when things are calm so you have something to rely on when it gets crazy, listening when you'd rather just power through to get things done, and patiently explaining to your staff why we do what we do for our customers. To get the time and energy to do this you must say no to the urgent things masquerading as important—the Busy-ness—and keep saying yes to those truly important activities.

Covey made the case for Investment over Busy-ness better than anyone. As he wrote, "You have to decide what your highest priorities are and have the courage—pleasantly, smilingly, non-apologetically—to say no to other things. And the way you do that is by having a bigger yes burning inside. The enemy of the best is often the good."[12]

Reduce the energy needed to get going

To help you get going on important activities, you can leverage the concept of activation energy that Shawn Achor introduced in his book *The Happiness Advantage*.[13] Activation energy is the not-to-exceed amount of effort and time it takes from thinking about to actually doing an activity. Surprisingly, the threshold is about 30 to 120 seconds for most people. For example, if it takes more than a minute or two in the morning to find and put your running clothes and shoes on, you're more likely to talk yourself into staying in bed. So when you identify important activities you want to do, make them easy to get started on within a minute. (Shawn tested this himself by sleeping in his running clothes with his shoes right next to the bed and found it made the difference between running and not most mornings.) Conversely, if you make less-important activities take longer than a minute to start, you'll likely find yourself doing them far less.

Exercise 2.1 | **What are you focusing on?**

Use this exercise to reflect on how importance and urgency are showing up in your life. Each part can be done separately. Each is designed to give you a chance to step back and evaluate how well you're focusing on those challenging and important activities for yourself as a leader.

1. **Shift a percentage of time you spend on urgent matters to more important things.** Take a few minutes and write down how you're spending your time. Now get the opinions of at least two other trusted people to validate. If you're not happy with the results, choose one item this week that is important yet not urgent, and commit to making that a priority. Once you start to see the important work you've done preventing fire drills, reinvest your recovered time in the next important and not urgent activity.

2. **Check the results you're seeking.** Take a few minutes and list the last three-to-five self-assigned projects. Note how much each builds capacity, relationships, and resilience of the organization, your people, and yourself. Note any patterns—positive or negative. Commit to shifting your focus on your next project to include at least one investment activity.

3. **Use activation energy to your advantage.** Pick one important activity that you can't seem to do. Brainstorm ways you could reduce the time and energy to get started on the activity to 30-120 seconds. Try one of these changes, and if that doesn't work, try another until you find what works for you.

Start small, and as your efforts bear positive results reinvest the time and energy you saved for even better results. It's amazing what my company's clients have been able to achieve—even as they felt completely overloaded—through shifting their thinking and commitments around importance versus urgency.

RISK AND BE RESILIENT

Practice 2.2 | **Risk and be resilient**

Ripple Leaders deal with the unknown first and then adapt to achieve the outcome.

Every leader experiences a time when, despite their best efforts, the organization doesn't seem to be making progress. Whenever we stop pushing, it slides back. Talk about frustrating! And yet, we may be doing this to ourselves.

Forward progress no matter the cost

I used to accompany my grandfather on rides to our family's Colorado mountain cabin up Buckhorn Canyon, near Rocky Mountain National Park. As he drove his rattly old four-wheel-drive Ford Bronco up the final winding logging road, there would often be large snowdrifts blocking our way. To get through the drifts, my grandfather would simply put the accelerator to the floor and hold it there.

We'd crash into the drift, engine screaming, wheels and tire-chains spinning, rocks and snow flying. The Bronco would slowly dig its way down to solid ground, leaping a few feet forward at a time. The process was repeated until we were through the drift, had to dig the Bronco out, or some mechanical part failed. I can remember many flat tires, a cracked engine block, and even a broken driveshaft. But no matter—we were going to make progress whatever the cost.

When I was able to drive myself, I could only afford a little Volkswagen station wagon that didn't have the power to go through the drifts. So I developed a different approach: I would look for the area of the drift with the least snow, gather some speed, and drive smoothly forward until my

This practice
is helpful if:

- **You find yourself living out "Groundhog Day"—experiencing the same challenges again and again with no relief or improvement.**

- **Employees do lots of could've/would've/ should've/second guessing.**

- **The organization is often "overcome by circumstances" where a decision is no longer needed since the situation dictates what must be done.**

wheels began to spin. Then I backed down the hill to where I could reapply power, stayed in the same tracks, got my speed back up, got further into the drift, and so on until I emerged on the other side. To succeed, I willingly backed down the hill to build up momentum for each new attempt.

During my years as a leadership consultant, I've noticed that many leaders reflexively stomp on the accelerator when they feel their business "slipping." They throw amazing effort, hours, and resources at the problem at hand. While this approach more often than not gets the organization through the problem, it can also exhaust resources, frazzle nerves, and break engine-level components, like commitment and enthusiasm.

Sometimes you need to back down to move forward

When you have a long-term perspective, it's much easier to focus on building momentum instead of forward progress at all costs. We can respond to problems by easing off the accelerator and allowing ourselves to move backwards while looking for the just the right spot to reapply effort. The repeated efforts that build on each other cannot only get us over the obstacle that's holding us up but also allow us to have a steady, controllable pace and get to our ultimate destination with people and resources intact. These are exactly the kinds of small changes rippling out from each stone you throw that can eventually add up to wash over a sea wall. And this cumulative effort can be far more impactful than hitting things head on.

You get what you focus on

I once worked with a group of hospitals headed by a CEO who was a very driven man. Such ambition for achieving high goals is generally a good thing. Yet this gentleman was driving his team crazy.

This CEO's dislike of failure was so intense that he would pounce on anything that looked even remotely like a problem. His staff quickly learned to do everything possible to avoid his involvement so they didn't have the dual task of dealing with the problem and the hands-on attention of the CEO. This led to the senior executive team members trying to solve systemic problems individually, which of course rarely worked. So the CEO would find out about failures only after they had already occurred. This sequence of events reinforced the CEO's belief that his people were incapable and that his involvement ferreting out problems was absolutely critical in preventing failures. When this hospital system merged with another, this well-intentioned yet overly driven gentleman was probably surprised to find himself suddenly out of a job. His fear of failure—of somehow not doing things right—led directly to his fear coming true. Better if he had allowed himself and his staff some leeway to be human.

Patricia Ryan Madson wrote a fabulous little book that most business people wouldn't look at even if someone handed it to them. Yet this treasure chest is so packed with great ideas, examples, and stories that my copy is a dog-eared mess. The book, *Improv Wisdom: Don't Prepare, Just Show Up*,[14] helps people embrace the reality that life is something we make up as we go along.

The maxims in the book remind us in playful ways to take risks. They invite us to:

- Say yes.
- Just show up.
- Start anywhere.
- Make mistakes, please.
- Act now.
- Enjoy the ride.

Have you ever worked for a leader unwilling to do some of the above? If so, I would bet your organization suffered in a futile effort to create a safe, predictable experience for that leader. Because at some point, real life will intrude. The regular pattern will be interrupted, and things won't go as planned. This is the point when the leader needs to step out into the unknown and improvise—maybe trying a different approach, a new method, or simply backing up until the organization is once again on firm

The riskiest thing possible is to try to eliminate risk.

ground. Unfortunately a leader who is unable to shift how he approaches challenges will quickly find his ability to effect positive growth melting away around him. Fortunately, organizations that suffer that kind of leadership eventually shake themselves free of that leader and find one who can more fully embrace necessary risks.

The good news is that taking risks also provides opportunities for change. And the more small and frequent risks you take, the more opportunities you have to adjust the path you are on.

A cabinetmaker I worked with once told me:

You have two choices — make it perfect or make it adjustable.

As often as possible, I work to make things adjustable—and then be sure to adjust as we go. This mindset applies to just about everything that needs to function in a changing world: house plans, employment agreements, contracts, even meeting agendas. Everything works better when it begins with a basic structure that can be changed as the need arises.

However, making something adjustable means that it needs to be used before it gets adjusted. Sadly, I see many teams of well-intentioned executive officers vigorously reworking plans and decisions that have never seen the light of day. They debate and argue, focusing on making things perfect from their perspective alone, trying to guess what might happen so they can prevent a problem before it occurs. The only thing they're preventing is getting something done (or, as Seth Godin likes to say, "shipped"). They are so worried about making a mistake they have forgotten an important truth:

*Real feedback only comes
as a response to real action.*

Until a plan hits the real world, feedback is simply conjecture. It may match reality. Then again, it may not.

How to deal with a big problem

In 2010, European airspace was closed for more than a week because of an ash cloud from an Icelandic volcano, stranding thousands of travelers and costing tremendous amounts of money. Some scary real-life situations from the past, together with some reasonable analysis, led people to predict that the ash could damage jet engines and possibly bring planes full of passengers crashing to the ground. However, after seeing the cost of inactivity skyrocketing, some airlines took it upon themselves to get actual feedback. They flew planes without passengers through the ash and carefully measured performance characteristics and engine-part impacts. The real feedback proved that there was virtually no negative effect from flying a commercial passenger jet through the ash. With this objective evidence, authorities turned the travel spigot back on.

With real feedback, effective adjustments are possible.

Exercise 2.2 | **How to get past the snow drifts without bogging down**

This set of exercises is designed to increase your own awareness about what's getting in your way and how you can build momentum to get to the outcomes you desire.

1. **Examine what you're tolerating.** Get a clean page in your notebook and write down what you're currently tolerating or working around in your business or personal life. Don't hold back. When you're done, look for patterns or commonalities. Underline the tolerations that are most getting in your way, or are causing resource intensive workarounds.

2. **Check out the part you're playing.** On that same sheet, write the "payoff" or benefit you derive from continuing to allow the significant tolerations. This requires a little mental gymnastics as we tend not to think of getting something good from tolerating a situation or problem. Frequently clients find that by tolerating a problem, their payoff is that they put off or avoid some other issue they perceive as bigger or thornier.

3. **Brainstorm what you could do differently.** Look at one thing you're tolerating and the payoff that may be helping you tolerate it. What could you do differently to get the same payoff and at the same time reduce or eliminate the thing you're tolerating? It might require backing down the hill a ways to get to firm footing before you head up the hill again. Or potentially getting out of your comfort zone—at least a little.

Whatever's in your way, the best plan is to pick the smallest possible effort you can make with the highest chance of success, and then implement that change. The goal is to keep your momentum up and get past whatever's getting in your way in the simplest way you can.

To sustain that momentum to carry you as far as possible, you'll need to make sure to keep your own energy and effectiveness up—no one else will do it for you.

CHARGE YOUR OWN BATTERIES

This practice is helpful if:

- **You find yourself burning the candle at both ends and the middle—with occasional illness forcing you to take time off.**

- **Employees are getting burnt out and are stepping down or leaving.**

- **The organization is going faster than anyone can keep up with.**

Practice 2.3 | **Charge your own batteries**

Caring for and strengthening yourself ensures effectiveness that makes Ripple Leadership possible.

Stephen R. Covey introduced me to the importance of personal renewal by telling a story about cutting wood. I have a similar story, which goes something like this:

Some people work harder; others work smarter

At sunrise one day a young man and an older man were headed into the forest to cut wood, axes on their shoulders. The young man, feeling a bit brash, challenged the older man to a contest.

"Let's have a little friendly competition to see who can cut the most wood, old-timer! Loser buys the winner a pint of beer. What do you say?"

The older fellow thought for a moment, then agreed with a handshake before walking to one side of the valley.

The younger man could almost taste the beer as he went straight to work on the other side of the valley, chopping away with vigorous, quick strokes. Before the sun had risen very high, he noticed the older man sitting down to take a rest. The young man laughed to himself as he continued chopping away and felling trees.

At noon, the young man again saw the old man sitting and resting. The young man grabbed some bread and continued working while chewing and smiling to himself about how good the beer would taste.

As the sun began to set, the young man finally looked up again and was astonished to see a larger pile of logs on the other side of the valley. He redoubled his effort before it got dark, but it was too late. He was clearly beaten.

When the sun finally dropped below the horizon, the two men began to walk back toward the town, the younger man trying to hide the disappointment on his face and soreness in his arms. As they neared the pub, the younger man could not hold back his frustration any longer and blurted out, "OK, old man. You've got that pint coming. But not before you tell me how you won. Every time I looked over you were sitting down, resting!"

The older man slowly smiled.

"You're right. You did see me sitting down during the day."

The younger man looked confused, so the older man went on.

"What you didn't see was that every time I sat down, I sharpened my axe."

Of course, if we modernized this contest today, it would probably involve two fellows on cellphones stuck in an airport closing deals. The wiser one would retreat to a seat with a power outlet every hour or so to charge his phone and win. The analogy doesn't matter as much as the lesson that only you can prevent your own burnout.

As a leader you may feel like you can't stop driving because some cruel joker fastened the accelerator pedal of the business to the floor. There is no off switch, no key to turn. You have no time to pull over and do something for yourself. All you can do is try to avoid obstacles and stay on the road. After all, so many people are relying on you. How could you even think of slowing down? Allow me to help a bit and reframe the question:

What happens if you're too busy driving to get gas?

Rest and renewal are critical parts of our rhythm as human beings. Besides nightly sleep, many cultures set aside time each week, month, and even year to refresh body and soul. Conventional wisdom, on the other hand, is to tough it out and keep going until you have to stop. Some CEOs and senior leaders will even brag about how little vacation, if any, they've taken in their roles, like it's a badge of honor and symbol of loyalty.

Mechanics will tell you that the gas at the bottom of the tank usually has enough accumulated crud to clog and damage the fuel system. How effective are you when you're running on fumes? You need not look further than our culture's high level of alcohol, caffeine, and energy-drink use to know that people are trying to cope with unnatural levels of stress in unnatural ways.

As a leader, regular renewal is essential to your effectiveness for two reasons. First, downtime enables you to be sharp and effective when you most need to be. Second, your personal sharpening sets the example for your people to do the same, which in turn promotes a greater capacity for everyone to work effectively and to respond to occasional surges of extra effort within your organization.

Exercise 2.3 | **Keep yourself sharp**

Paying attention to where you are spending energy, and also giving yourself permission to invest time, energy, and resources into your own well-being, are key to keeping yourself the best tool in your toolbox.

1. **Take stock of where you are right now.** Take a few minutes and write down in your notebook how you are doing: Where are the same personal results taking more effort? Where is the same effort giving you worse results? What do these mean about your own personal sharpness mentally, emotionally, physically, and spiritually?

2. **Get out your whetstone.** Take a few minutes, show your significant other or trusted friend your results from step 1 above, and ask this person what you could do for yourself that you are not doing now. Pick one doable, promising thing from their suggestions or your own ideas, and get into action.

3. **Cultivate a habit of living your life in gratitude.** Spend one minute each night jotting down three things that you are grateful for that day. Recent research[15] has shown this single action is more effective than psychoactive drugs to help people deal with depression and unhappiness. Over time you will begin to feel less resistance to the changes you decide to make in your life.

Self-renewal is a habit that can make the difference between burning up your candle from both ends, and being able to shine a light continuously to help other people see where to go.

How are you in action around your personal responsibilities as a leader?

The action orientation of a leader can make the difference between making things happen and allowing circumstances to rule. This simple assessment can help you see how well you understand yourself in relation to the practices we just covered.

Look at each set of statements and mentally mark an X where you are on the continuum of that practice. Think of this more as a baseline than a report card. And don't cheat yourself. Dishonest assessments are not valuable to you.

Where are you right now on the following practices?

Practice 2.1 | **Do the hard stuff**

I do what's in front of me in the moment	I focus on and always do what's most important	I have no patience for anything but what's most important to me

Practice 2.2 | **Risk and be resilient**

I do what's easy and practical	I constantly challenge myself to do better	I get bored if I'm not taking bet-the-farm risks

Practice 2.3 | **Charge your own batteries**

My body better keep up with my schedule	I take care of my body, mind, and spirit	I spend most of my time improving myself

Consider these questions...

- Which practice stands out as important and urgent for you to address?

- How will working on it help you, others, and the organization?

- What's holding you back from working on it?

Important points about leading yourself

Reflection and repetition allow us to learn lessons from what we've already heard, read, and done. Here's a summary of the important points from the section on Leading Yourself:

Principle 1

Leaders' effectiveness is proportional to how well they know themselves.

Decide what matters most

Your personal values are the best compass for your unique journey.

Chart your own course

Picturing your own personal future helps you see what steps to take— or not—to get there.

Know where you're awesome

People often don't recognize their own strengths—and you cannot tap what you do not know.

Principle 2

Leaders are judged more by what they don't than by what they do.

Do the hard stuff

Doing what's most important is the hardest and most rewarding work you will do as a leader.

Risk and be resilient

Leaders deal with the unknown first—and then must adjust to achieve the outcome.

Charge your own batteries

Caring for and strengthening yourself ensures effectiveness that makes your leadership possible.

CREATE RIPPLES
BY LEADING OTHER(S)

The ability to get results beyond what you can do personally flows directly from how much you help and positively enable others. This ability is at the core of all leaders.

Some leaders view their followers or staff merely as a way to accomplish their own agenda. For example, most organizational charts include lines of authority flowing downward from the top of the pyramid, illustrating some sort of power bestowed from above. That model may have worked for the organizations of yesterday, but today's organizations succeed only by securing, motivating, and utilizing the talents of others.

Getting people to give their best—for free

Look no further than the example of Wikipedia. Thousands of contributors willingly invest their precious time and best efforts—with no pay and little recognition—to provide detailed information on just about any topic you can imagine.[16] The small paid staff provides support, gives direction, and helps enforce the standards everyone commits to in this vast voluntary workforce. There is no way Wikipedia's results could happen using the traditional top-down, you're-not-paid-to-think model of leadership. The future rests in the hands of leaders who attract and inspire people to contribute their best selves to the work that needs to be done.

Leadership begins with how you treat each and every person, every single day. It's that simple—and that difficult.

In Leading Other(s), there are two principles that are key to your success as a Ripple Leader:

> **Principle 3—People discover their best selves through being respected by a leader.** Through respect, you can establish trust, understanding, and belief in each person you work with.

Ripple Leadership is about getting other people to willingly work on the goal you believe needs to be accomplished.

Principle 4—People multiply a leader's power only as much as that power is shared. You are responsible for challenging, equipping, and growing each person you work with.

You may wonder why I use "Other(s)." It's to get your attention, because your collective success is determined by how you respect and enable *every single person* in your organization. It's not the group that makes things happen, although group dynamics can certainly play a part. Each individual relationship is vital to a leader's success—not just those that connect the leader and followers.

Unfortunately, many leaders see and treat their team as a blob of human needs and potential. The Team starts to seem like an entity rather than a diverse group of people. The antidote to this perspective is for the leader to focus his or her perspective on each person as an individual, which then leads the other members of the team to do the same and enables the unique value each person can add.

How to build organizational resiliency through relationships

Imagine 10 people standing in a circle with the appointed leader at the center. Now imagine everyone having a piece of rope connecting him or her with the leader, symbolizing each relationship.

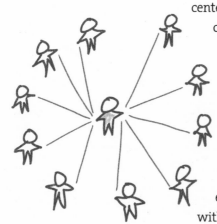

With this arrangement, when the leader pulls on someone's rope, that person responds. Simple cause and effect. As the leader understands what is needed from the group, she will pull the right ropes at the right times, which then should cause the right things to happen. Structurally, the team is loyal and responsive. Yet the team's success is limited by the leader's abilities and mere existence. This model has its applications, especially for organizations that are just starting out. But it comes with a potentially fatal flaw—a single point of failure.

If the leader leaves or is replaced, then all 10 ropes drop and the group is plunged into confusion, not knowing how to respond. Competition erupts as some or all of the remaining members of the team position themselves to become the next leader at the center. I've personally seen this again and again—when a strong leader leaves a team, members fall into disarray because they have essentially been trained by the leader simply to respond to pulls on their own rope.

The relationship model I work with my clients to create looks similar yet is substantially different. Imagine the same group of 10 people with the leader taking an important position on the rim of the circle instead of in the center. As before, the leader actively initiates and strengthens relationships with each individual person. Yet in this model, the leader is not relying solely on his or her authority to make or break the effectiveness of the team. That power is instead shared with the team simply by having the leader present in the rim in a role equally important and simply different from the other roles on the team.

The strength of this shared power multiplies as the leader encourages everyone else to build strong relationships with everyone around them. Through leading by example, the leader here cultivates a web of over 50 relationships to grow among the team, connecting them all and creating a woven net that is the team's strength.

Not only is this team strong, loyal, and responsive, it is significantly more resilient than those forged using the leader-centric model. Why? Because if the leader has to step away, while 10 ropes would drop, more than 40 would remain to take up the load and support the group's purpose. You can see this by comparing the sketches on this page and the next. Detecting the difference of 10 fewer ropes is rather difficult.

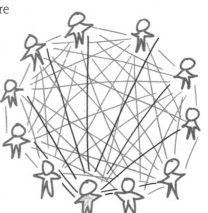

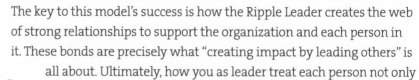

The key to this model's success is how the Ripple Leader creates the web of strong relationships to support the organization and each person in it. These bonds are precisely what "creating impact by leading others" is all about. Ultimately, how you as leader treat each person not only makes a significant difference for that one person, but also has the potential to enable everyone else that one person connects with. The impact of each action you take to build relationships creates ripples that reverberate around the organization, further energizing everyone in it.

As you build each of the many one-on-one relationships in your team, you will be more successful if you are aware of how your role itself affects those relationships. And you probably underestimate the impact you already have.

It's a big challenge for leaders to really understand the impact they have on other people beyond their intentions. To help clarify that impact in the minds of my clients, I developed an analogy that allows the unintentional consequences of their actions to be understood, regardless of their seniority level, department, or organizational size.

The Leadership Fishbowl

Let's imagine for a moment that your role can be represented by a large glass fishbowl. This fishbowl is of the old fashioned variety: hand-blown with lots of wavy spots and distortions in the glass.

Everyone else in your organization is outside the fishbowl. This fishbowl moves with you so you don't even notice it's there. And all your interactions with others are affected by this fishbowl in two ways:

1. People outside the fishbowl will misinterpret your intentions

As a leader, you have great intentions. However other people can't see intentions through the fishbowl. They can only make out your actions, and those actions can be distorted at best. This leads people to assume what your real intentions are—and people usually assume a worst-case scenario. Thanks to such improper assumptions, you can suddenly find yourself dealing with a reality that you never intended to create.

For example, a fellow I know founded a start-up where everyone in the company interviewed every prospective employee. As CEO, he was completely committed to a culture of collective effort and teamwork. This policy worked pretty well—until they were at 30 people and their VP of Marketing suddenly left due to a family situation. They needed serious marketing help fast! He remembered his buddy from college who majored in marketing, hired him over a weekend, and introduced him to the company on Tuesday morning as the new VP of Marketing. However, his message hit the side of the fishbowl and got completely distorted. Even though his intentions were good—get quick, effective, and trusted marketing help right away—you can probably guess how everyone outside the fishbowl interpreted the message:

- It's not what you do, it's who you know.
- My opinion no longer is important.
- The boss doesn't care about me or the team.
- I don't matter here anymore.

In the aftermath of hiring the new VP, the business went into a tailspin. Productivity went down and Internet use went up as people started checking out other opportunities. When the CEO noticed this and started probing a bit, he discovered that the fishbowl was also preventing good communication coming in.

2. **Feedback from people outside the fishbowl can feel like a personal attack**

When something is noted as being less than good from outside your leadership fishbowl, as it passes through the fishbowl it focuses into a

How you treat each person significantly impacts everyone in the organization.

white-hot laser beam that hits you right in the chest! Even though the information is simply how others are perceiving the situation at hand, the fishbowl causes this information to feel like a personal attack on you and what you are working so hard to accomplish.

Take again the start-up founder who pushed a new VP of Marketing on his team. When one brave soul shared that she felt her opinion didn't matter anymore, he exploded back on her:

> "What? Now, let's be fair here. We're talking ONE PERSON! One...out of thirty! Up to now, I've let you pick and choose every single person on the team. Don't I get to make decisions about the makeup of this team? Didn't I build this company from scratch?"

You can see how these two problems can combine to create a "non-feedback" loop: First, someone casually mentions, "I think we could be better in [business component]." Second, the comment passes into the fishbowl, concentrating like a laser beam that strikes the responsible leader in the chest. Third, the leader takes it personally and reacts in a non-objective manner. Fourth, this reaction— as seen from outside the fishbowl—is interpreted by everyone as the leader being unable to handle any bad news. After some time, the leader is left wondering why he or she never knows about failures until they are occurring or have occurred.

The good news is that the remedy to these problems is simple.

For communication that's heading out to others, share what you intend or want to happen, and also add a contrasting statement about what you don't intend or want to happen. To do this, imagine how your message could be misunderstood from outside the fishbowl. What message might the listeners receive if they didn't assume positive intent? Then in your communication, make sure to directly address both what you want and whatever incorrect negative story will pop into your listeners' minds. In the real-life situation above, the CEO would have benefited by saying, "I want to get us immediate help for marketing, and I want to make sure you know that you really matter here." If he shared this beforehand, his team would know where he was coming from and also have a chance to contribute suggestions to resolve the problem.

For communication that's coming into the fishbowl, assume positive intent and don't take it personally. This is easier said than done, yet by not taking feedback or criticism personally, you can stay unemotional and ask questions that help you understand and apply the other person's perspective to the problem. Again, using the situation where the brave person told the CEO that she felt her opinion didn't matter, a better response would have been, "Wow. I definitely don't want you to feel that way. Your opinion matters a lot to me. Can you tell me more?" (You may notice a little contrasting here as well.)

The rest of the real-life story? With a little coaching, the leader was able to calm down, share his real intent, and then listen to what people were feeling. He ended up promising that everyone would indeed interview the new marketing VP and if anyone objected strongly to his decision, he would change it. With the path now cleared, everyone interviewed the VP and positively confirmed that the CEO had made an excellent choice.

Using contrasting statements to improve your communication takes practice. Consider this next exercise to help you become more aware of the ripples you're making and to begin changing the way you affect others.

Exercise 3.0 | **Deal with your fishbowl**

To minimize the impact of distortion around your role, you'll need to become more aware how it's affecting you and others. Then you can begin improving the clarity of communication and perception of others on the outside.

1. **Check for distortion outside the fishbowl.** Take a few minutes and make a list in your notebook of the last several times you were misunderstood. If you can't recall any, find a trusted advisor—the kind of person who would tell you if you had spinach in your teeth—and ask them to share any times when what you said didn't make sense to someone. Look for any patterns to help you start seeing where and how your messages may be getting distorted.

2. **Check for scorch marks inside the fishbowl.** Take a few minutes and make another list in your notebook of last few times you reacted strongly to an update or news from others. Where might you be taking things too personally? Imagine positive intent and then see if and where the messages shift for you in meaning. Note any patterns that emerge.

3. **Pull out the glass polish.** With both lists in mind, take a few more minutes and project the patterns forward to your next probable encounter. Are there some challenges brewing? Is there something you are extra-sensitive about that is likely to come up? Jot down a quick script of how you want to do things differently to achieve different and better results. Then be proactive and initiate some better communication.

Keep practicing—you'll get credit from people even for attempts that don't end perfectly. When people understand your full intent, and they believe you see their intent as positive, your fishbowl will be so shiny and clear hardly anyone will even notice it's there.

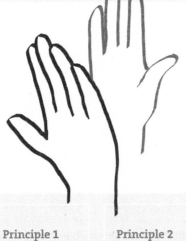

Principle 3

People discover their best selves through being respected by a leader

Principle 1
Leaders'
effectiveness
is proportional
to how well
they know
themselves

Principle 2
Leaders are
judged more
by what they
don't than by
what they do

Principle 4
People
multiply a
leader's power
only as much
as that power
is shared

Principle 5
Organizations
are designed
to get the
results they
are getting

Principle 6
Organizations
generating
waste are
generating
opportunities
for improve-
ment

Principle 3

People discover their best selves through being respected by a leader

If you've experienced the respect of a great teacher, you know what a difference it can make in your life. For me, that difference came through Mrs. Kramer.

A lifeline in the stormy sea of puberty

Sixth grade was one of the hardest times in my life. I'd grown eight inches over the summer to six feet tall, and yet at just 110 pounds, I was the proverbial beanpole. My family had just moved back from living overseas for five years, which made me culturally illiterate around fashions, television shows...you name it. At the exact time when everyone was seeking conformity to avoid being singled-out and picked on by someone else, I stuck out. I arrived at a small school in Northern Virginia a few days after school had already started and met the teacher whose respect would help transform me into who I am today.

Mrs. Kramer was tall—nearly the same height as me—with red hair and a great smile. She looked right past my shortcomings and saw greatness I didn't even know existed. When she realized I had already completed all the sixth-grade material, she brought in her own college literature and math books. I read *Flowers for Algernon* and *The Secret Life of Walter Mitty*. I took inventory of our school supplies and put together her supply requests each month. I balanced her personal checkbook. I read stories every day to kindergartners in the library. Mrs. Kramer even took me to

Leaders who listen, look for, and uncover others' strengths create capacity and commitment.

attend a political rally when I was learning about government. My confidence blossomed even as my voice began to crack.

Mrs. Kramer didn't have to care about me, or create a curriculum to stretch my learning, or even ask questions about what I enjoyed and what I was learning. It's exactly because she took the interest, time, and effort to respect me in a deeper way that I was able to better understand my own potential and become motivated to reach for it. She created a ripple that's lasted a very long time and has probably impacted thousands of people. How would you like for someone to be praising you in writing 35 years after you worked with her?

We all have an amazing capacity to be tremendously loving or tremendously inhumane to other people. There's plenty of evidence of both in the world. Choosing between the two is one of our most fundamental choices, and it is up to us as leaders to choose the stone and throw it just so to optimize the positive ripples from the impact of our interactions with others.

To help you respect people deeply, there are five practices in the third principle of Ripple Leadership:

1. *Trust or have nothing.* Like oil in an engine, with trust things run well. Without it you get friction and struggle.

2. *Mission first. People second. You? Last.* You need to be able to put others' need before yours.

3. *Assume most of your stories are wrong.* Prejudging others' intentions and abilities limits you both more than you realize.

4. *Look for diamonds in the dirt.* Helping others see their own strengths allows their greatness to shine.

5. *Help them figure out how to fish.* Create ownership by asking questions that help others struggle and grow.

Each of these practices build on one another to create a strong and healthy relationship between you and every person you lead. They might seem like common sense, yet it's amazing to me how people choose instead to create relationships with others that are superficial and dictatorial.

But it's just business, right?

How many times have you heard an executive being inhumane to someone and then saying, "Don't take it personally. It's just business."? Every time I hear that line, it rings in my ears as an excuse for not being a real leader. I have participated in several strategic business resets in my working life that did result in people losing their jobs. In those that were handled with respect and dignity, everyone involved understood and appreciated the company making the best of a bad situation. Sadly, I've also seen people in leadership positions who treated people with less respect than they deserved—more like interchangeable cogs in a machine than human beings.

In tough times, respect may be all you can give

I once worked for a large division of a tech company that experienced significant challenges due to market conditions and, frankly, a few bad business decisions that caused significant waves in the organization. This organization shipped production overseas to reduce costs, then discovered that production didn't work so well when the engineers and production personnel weren't able to discuss problems over lunch in the cafeteria. This caused further turmoil, so the executive team decided to find an acquisition to buoy the business in the raging storm.

The acquisition turned out to be a leaky balloon, as the product wasn't really ready for production, the customer base had not paid for any of the units they were using, and the technical staff was inexperienced. Rumors of layoffs reverberated throughout the organization (nothing creates a bigger ripple than a rumor!), and morale dropped through the floor. Then I got called into a special meeting in which all managers were informed which positions were being eliminated.

To lay off my staff, I was instructed to report to a conference room with a short script in hand and to keep my mouth shut. Human Resources (HR) would do all the talking and cue me to say my lines. I reported as ordered to an empty conference room, when an employee walked in with a puzzled look, sat down, and asked, "So...why are we here?" No HR in sight. My mind instantly scrambled for small talk—and then stopped. There was no way I could be anything but direct and honest. I stood up, closed the door, looked this longtime and loyal employee straight in the eye, and spoke from my heart. "I'm very sorry. Your position has been eliminated, and this meeting is to give you details about the process and your next steps." His eyes widened as he went into shock. I continued, "I don't have any more information than that, and I trust HR will be here shortly. I wish things were different." We sat there quietly for several minutes, him looking ashen and lost, me trying to hold him up with my thoughts. Finally, the HR representative came in, and I said "He knows why we're here." She nodded, sat down, and began walking him through how his life would be different going forward.

Had I followed my instruction sheet and simply chatted with this man before HR showed up to lay him off, I would have been "professional" and "business-like." Instead, I simply thought about how I would want to be treated and did that. Later on that day I stopped by his office as he was packing up. He looked a bit bleary, yet he gave me a solid handshake, looked me in the eye, paused, and said, "Thanks." It probably wasn't our senior leadership's intent to treat this process like a conveyor belt, and while I didn't want to be there, I was glad I could provide him some respect.

Ripple Leaders know the difference between dealing with a difficult situation by throwing bucketfuls of stones at the water versus smoothly and effectively launching one stone at a time for an impact that's as respectful of each person as possible. It's exactly when the situation is screaming at you to do the wrong thing that doing the right thing has the greatest impact.

Every human desires respect. In our fast-paced society today, we are bombarded with messages about how we will be respected for the material possessions we have, or for how many people know about us, or for how much influence we have over others.

The problem is that many people believe that getting possessions and celebrity and power are the path to respect, instead of being the fruits of living a life respecting others. Leaders who focus exclusively on one or more of these without respecting others will eventually find themselves in "leadership bankruptcy," when they become embroiled in a scandal, in jail, or worse.

These people have not yet learned that you get what you project. What you do to other people is what they will tend to do back to you. In other words:

The best way to be respected
is to be respectful

Remember—the stones you toss create ripples, some of which come back to you. Consciously deciding what kind of impact you want for others and yourself can help you figure out which of the following practices can help you achieve that impact.

**This practice
is helpful if:**

- You find others
delaying doing
what you ask, subtly
undermining, or even
overtly engaging
against your efforts.

- Employees are
behaving badly—from
not speaking directly
about problems, to
working around certain
people, to even walking
out of meetings or
threatening others
(usually done
defending their
function to hide
personal animosity).

- The organization
moves forward at a
snail's pace with great
expense of energy,
work, and money.
Schedules are slipped,
budgets run over,
sales are missed, and
good people leave for
greener pastures.

Practice 3.1 | **Trust or have nothing**

**Like oil in an engine, trust makes everything run well. Without it you
get friction and struggle.**

With trust, friction is low, effort is easy, and speed is high. All the energy
used goes toward creating forward motion together. Systems and people
who have built-in trust are like a perpetual-energy machine. They can run
smoothly for as long as they wish.

Without trust, friction is high, effort can be extreme, and speed is
intermittent and challenging to maintain. All the energy is used up in the
process and creates tremendous amounts of heat and noise, which in turn
can permanently damage the people and systems trying to do the work.

With trust, people don't need to protect themselves because others "have
their back." They don't need to posture because it's OK to say, "I made
a mistake." They get both the result they are looking for and stronger
relationships at work.

Without trust, the only person that matters is me, and organizations
become collections of individual islands, working alone in the same
building.

Many people think of trust as a "nice-to-have." However, I have yet to see a
successful long-term business or personal relationship without trust at its
center.

Interestingly, one of the myths around trust is that either you have it or
you don't. While trust can be destroyed in seconds, it can also be built,
with courage and intentional effort.

Building trust with a new client

For example, one of my clients is a smart and successful CEO who founded a national construction and remodeling company. He personally negotiated nearly every significant deal his company made. He wanted to grow his company, and he realized that getting an outside perspective and assistance was a good way to accelerate growth.

He and I worked together to create a program that would help grow the vision and capacity of his executive team. Once we agreed on the diagnosis and methods, we worked on the investment of time and money it would take for us to do the project. After some back and forth, we agreed on a consulting fee that worked for both of us.

I thought we were done when he said, "Oh, just one more thing. I'd like you to cover the travel." This was about ten percent of the cost and represented a fair amount of my company's planned profit. "And I'd like a ten-percent holdback," he added.

I felt a little like a waiter who, upon presenting the meal a customer ordered, was asked for a different price. Yet our relationship was just in its infancy, and I knew my client wasn't exactly sure he would get what we were agreeing to.

After a short pause I said, "I believe there's considerable positive impact we'll create by working together, and I'm willing to pay for the travel as an investment in our relationship. Can you help me understand the holdback?"

He went on to explain that it was his practice to hold back a percentage of consultants' fees to ensure their performance, and that typically he held back 40 percent—so only ten percent was actually a sign of trust. As long as he got the results we were looking for, the final ten percent would be something like a bonus for my company at the end of the program.

I pondered this for a few moments, and then I shared my concerns as respectfully as I could.

"I'm a little worried that we could put the entire project at risk for this small amount. Most of the business owners I work with are very challenged to free up the time that's needed to get the results they want. I am concerned that by choosing not to engage in the process, you would get something of a bonus: you would get back your valuable time and a ten-percent discount on the project. Yet in actuality, we would be sacrificing the results we both want for a small savings."

Because I was trusting, and because this gentleman is a man of character, he completely saw my point. He immediately suggested a modification to the agreement. If we agreed I had not done my part, I would continue to help until the project was complete, and if he did not do his part, I would be paid the holdback at the project's end. I made the changes and sent the document to him for final approval.

"Just one more thing," I added. "Now that we're fully agreed, I just want to let you know that I don't believe a holdback will change my behavior in any way. I am completely committed to doing the right thing by you and your company regardless of the financial consequences to me. If I wasn't, I really shouldn't be in this business."

Nearly a year later we wrapped up that project and were negotiating another phase of work together when I asked him about the amount to be held back. He waved his hand. "No holdback," he smiled. "Not needed."

Clearly he needed to build trust in my character and my ability to deliver what I said I would do. By trusting him and myself, I was able to open a door we both could walk through together.

Exercise 3.1 | **To trust or not to trust, that is the question**

As a leader, you get what you project. So, to be respected, you must genuinely respect others. Don't trust blindly, but do show vulnerability and a willingness to admit that you could use some help. Until you do, you won't get that same openness from others. This exercise is focused on increasing your conscious awareness of the yin-yang of trust and control.

1. **Do a trust check.** Take a few minutes and write a list in your notebook of the people you work with and for, and rate yourself on a 0 to 10 scale on how trusting you are with each person. Be honest. Note any similarities or patterns in how you trust (or distrust).

2. **Do a control check.** Take a few minutes and reflect on the level of control versus trust you have in others. (You can use the list from the trust check.) Typically, the more a leader is controlling, the less he or she is trusting. Note these as well.

3. **Verify your results.** Take a few minutes and ask three people how much they think you trust them, also on a 0 to 10 scale. This would start out something like, "I'm noticing that sometimes I get so focused on results I might be coming across as not trusting or over-controlling. Would you be willing to help provide me some honest feedback? My goal is to build trust with you, not tear it down." After they rate you, you might ask for a specific example to help you understand. Thank them, then privately compare and contrast their numbers with the trust ratings you gave them.

4. **Start making deposits.** (OK, this is an investment, yet it's worth it.) Stephen Covey used the analogy of a bank account, except this account holds the amount of trust you have from another person. Look for opportunities to make trust deposits whenever possible: apologize when you've made a mistake; help the other person avoid problems; ask for assistance when you need it; and admit your shortcomings. These actions all build trust and can make a positive difference in your relationship.

Challenging yourself to be more trusting sets the example and provides the environment for others to show you more trust as well. Without trust, there is really no relationship for you to rely on when you need to ask people to step up to help you and the organization.

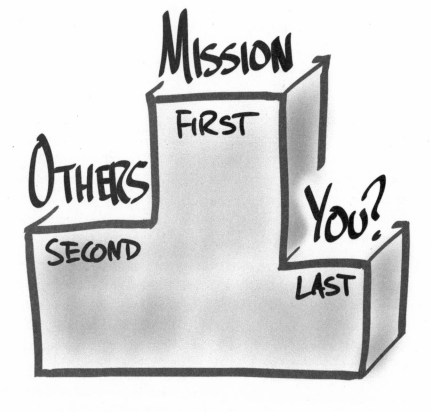

Practice 3.2 | **Mission first. People second. You? Last.**

You need to be able to put others' needs before yours.

Many people assume putting the needs of others ahead of their own means giving up and giving in. They think if you consider others' needs, you are broadcasting weakness and a desire to be taken advantage of. You might as well lie down and let them walk all over you.

Nothing could be further from the truth.

If done correctly, placing the needs of others first can be one of the most successful ways to partner with them and get your needs met at the same time. Ideally you help them see how what you want is aligned with what they want, so you can both put your shoulders to whatever's getting in the way of your joint success.

Staying aligned with a challenging boss

One of my clients was a senior executive who had been told by his CEO that he was next in line for the top position in the successful, growing company. Over time, however, a conflict arose between these two men. They became locked together in something of a power struggle, and it wasn't looking good for my client. No one at that company had lasted longer than a few months after a tussle with the boss.

The pressure my client was under began to "squirt out" in not-so-helpful ways. He snapped at people he saw as slowing things down, muttered comments under his breath during meetings, and dragged his feet on assignments he didn't think were valid.

This practice is helpful if:

- You find people responding to your requests with "What's in it for me / my team?"

- Employees are either vocal about getting their needs met, or say what they need to say to then do whatever they want.

- The organization rebuffs internal and external customers—pays them lip service and takes care of itself first. Customers stay only as long as they feel they don't have an option, and bad-mouth the company when asked about you.

My client's focus was fixed on the apparent shortcomings of the boss: Too controlling. Too mercurial. Decisions either made on a whim or declined even after being presented reams of data.

I could tell quickly that the best place to start would be to help him shift his perspective about whose needs came first. We talked about what worked for him when people needed something from him. He said he worked best with those who had his best interests at heart. Those who made his job easier.

"Let me check... From your boss' perspective, do you think you are making his job harder or easier?" I asked.

"Hmmm...probably not easier," he said. So together we started exploring one way of living out the practice of putting the mission first and others' needs second. I call this the Cascading Needs Process.

How to get other people's help to help the organization

The Cascading Needs Process takes just three simple steps to align your needs with others and the mission—and create positive ripples for everyone involved.

First, seek a shared, high-level objective. What is an important shared goal that makes sense for both of you to work to achieve? Look at your mission or purpose if you get stumped. The best objective is something that the other person is personally proud of or strongly connected to.

In this case we came up with the joint goal of creating an organization that serves as an example of what's possible as a socially, environmentally, and financially successful business.

You should move to the next step only when the other person is in full agreement with your common objective. The person needs to show interest and ideally should state the objective in his or her own words.

Some questions that might help with this phase of the process:

- What common objective do you both passionately believe in?

- What is your company's vision / mission / purpose?

- What achievements have you sensed you were both happy with?

- What things has the other person talked about or done that you really agree with?

Next, share what you believe the other person most needs to reach that objective. Ideally you won't just be talking about any particular project—you'll be speaking to the unspoken needs of the other party. This is incredibly powerful because it allows the other person to see that you have their needs in mind. You will create great energy if you can articulate needs they demonstrate yet have not specifically asked for. You're looking to get the other person leaning forward in the direction you both agree on.

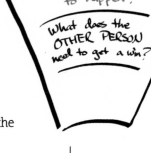

In this case my client and I determined that his boss needed to believe that things were going the right direction without being burdened with making those things happen. And the boss needed to get frequent updates and opportunities to tweak and approve the direction of activities.

Here are some questions that might help you discern the needs of the other person more clearly:

- If you took everything the person did and put it in a pile, what would be the most common thing you would see?

- What does the other person consistently strive to get for the organization? For themselves?

- What does the other person ask from you on a regular basis?

- What does the other person avoid?

- What are the other person's pet peeves?

If the other person lights up and gets much more interested in what you are saying, you've probably correctly diagnosed his or her needs.

Remember to move forward only when you get positive verbal agreement from the other person.

Finally, **ask for what you need to achieve the objective and meet the other person's needs.** The idea here is that you have alignment of goals and the other person understands you have their best interests in mind so now you can ask for the resources, authority, freedom, and feedback to ensure success.

In this case my client and I brainstormed until we figured out that he needed to have more authority and latitude to operate within the business to achieve the business goals. And there was a new emerging area within the business that he was very passionate about. We came up with a plan to propose a lateral move into a new position in this new area which didn't threaten the CEO, and provided a place for my client to thrive.

To prepare yourself to ask for what you need (in line with the mission and other person's needs, of course), here are a few questions:

- What's frustrating you or preventing you from being successful?

- What would make a tremendous difference to your ability to get things done?

- How much authority or autonomy do you need?

- What resources have you assumed you could not get?

- What have other people suggested or recommended would make you more successful?

- How could the other person see what you need as realistic and enable a win for them?

The reason this process works so well is it meets the deeper need for people to figure out "what's in it for me?" To get a sense of this, imagine if my client came in and applied this in the reverse order:

"Boss, I need my own position in a new area. I really need some control over what I'm doing. Why? Well, I know you need to control and review my work to make sure I'm on track, and I know you're doing it because our mission is to be successful, but I have to tell you, it's just not working for me."

You can tell that this approach wouldn't go too well. Same needs, yet in the wrong order they communicate self-centeredness and lack of understanding of the big picture.

My client did secure the new position and is passionately helping the business expand, in partnership with the CEO. In fact, more than one person has privately told my client that the fact he is still there gives them confidence that they, too, will be able to continue to grow and help the company even if they run into conflict with the boss.

By the way, while my example was leading upward to the CEO, the same approach is highly effective with peers or followers. If you've ever had a leader take the time to consider and validate your personal understanding of joint success and your needs when initiating a new project, making changes internally or shifting direction of the organization, you know the power of Mission first. Others second. Leader last.

RIPPLE | Practice 3.2: **Mission first. People second. You? Last.**

97

Exercise 3.2 | **Align your needs with others and the business**

This practice can make discussions with anyone from unhelpful customer service personnel to upset significant others go more smoothly. Start small and build on your successes.

1. **Use a Cascading Needs Process for a minor conflict you're currently dealing with.** Take a few minutes and write down answers to the questions above for each of the three steps of the process. Ask a trusted advisor for help if you get stuck trying to clarify the needs of the other person. Remember, the best answers are those that touch on unspoken yet demonstrated needs.

2. **Try it on for size.** Take five minutes (yes, it is that simple) and walk through the process with the person from start to finish. Script out the process if you want, and if the other person says, "Hey, are you trying something on me?", you can say, "Yes, I'm trying out a way to make sure what I'm doing is meeting your needs and the needs of the business."

Lather. Rinse. Repeat. Look for other opportunities to try out this process. The more you align your needs with others', the more they will see you as a resource to get where they and the organization need to go.

Assume Most of Your Stories Are **WRONG**

This practice is helpful if:

- You find yourself mentally writing people off—or worse, complaining to people about someone else's limitations.

- Employees seem to put people "in a box"—limiting their potential to what they have seen or assumed they have seen.

- The organization is complacent—settling for "what is" in terms of performance.

Practice 3.3 | **Assume most of your stories are wrong**

Prejudging another's intentions limits both of you more than you realize.

"I've been thinking this for a long time and I'll finally say it out loud. All **you** people need a lot more teamwork." —a C-level executive

One of the most persistent and powerful problems leaders face is believing their own stories. Case in point: the C-level executive who said the quote above with complete seriousness at a teambuilding session.

Leaders face challenges with their perception of self and others. We call this our blind spot—those situations where our own limited perception or judgmental biases get in the way of what's actually occurring. This process involves four steps, illustrated below, going from the experience we have, and then to the meaning we assign, the emotions that are triggered, and the resulting action we take. This is based on the model from *Crucial Conversations.*[17]

Four Steps from Experience to Action

This process is unconscious and automatic, yet by understanding it we can have more conscious control and thereby get better results.

Step 1. We **experience our environment** with our senses, which provide information about what is happening around us.

Step 2. We **assign meaning** to our experiences, and this is where the trouble begins.

Step 3. Once we've told ourselves a story, built on our sensory experience but also bundled with whatever story we have about the intent and character of the people involved, we **experience an emotional reaction**. While that reaction is sometimes positive, most often the ancient wiring that helped our ancestors survive by assuming the worst zaps us with a negative, fear-based reaction.[19]

Step 4. As the wave of negative emotional reaction goes through us, we feel compelled to **take action** to reduce the threat. Our action may be nuanced or dramatic, preparing us to fight the threat or take flight away from the problem.

The place to intervene in this process is in Step 2—the assignment of meaning—before our emotions which come from our lizard-brain defense mechanisms—carry us away.[20] And before we start seeing what we want to see.

Why? Because once a story (positive or negative) about an experience takes root, our brains start filtering out observed information that doesn't agree with this predefined internal story. This bias reinforces the story with every mental telling, perpetuating a cycle where good gets better and bad gets worse. On the good end of the spectrum, this is known as the Halo Effect.

How the Fundamental Attribution Error gets in our way

Our attempt to accurately assign meaning is waylaid by a phenomenon called Fundamental Attribution Error,[18] also known as Observer Bias. This psychological condition occurs when we as observers, intimately knowing our own situations, tend to assign blame for bad things that happen to us on the situation we're dealing with. However, if bad things happen to others, we tend to first assume flaws in the characters of those involved, and we don't fully consider the situations they are dealing with.

We do this because we experience our situation firsthand and are blind to the battles other people are fighting. Yet we can clearly see where they are coming up short, while our own failings are in our blind spot. As a side benefit, attributing our difficulties to our circumstances allows us to offload responsibility for what happened.

Conversely, when good things happen to us, the same Fundamental Attribution Error has us believing that the positive results are a reward for our good character. And when others get good results, we tend to brush off their accomplishments, concluding those things happened due to luck.

When we evaluate people by how we judge them

The Halo Effect[21] is where people tend to assign positive attributes to actions performed by someone they already think well of. The inverse is equally likely; people tend to assign negative attributes to anyone they don't believe is worthy. Either way, the observer discredits new information that doesn't fit with his previous story. For example, you may hear a person describe someone's success as a "fluke" if the observer has already made a negative conclusion about that person. Or you may hear a person defend the bad attitude or mistake of someone she likes with a casual "she must be having a bad day" dismissal.

One way to tell if you are telling yourself an inaccurate story

When you see or hear something and you feel your emotions surge strongly, there's a very good chance you are telling yourself a story. While it's possible your emotions are justified, the probability is higher that you are simply reacting to an incorrect, preconceived story that doesn't accurately reflect the circumstances. The cure to this bias is to ask a question that explores your understanding of the situation before your emotions take over.

> When you feel the flash of righteous indignation is exactly the moment to stop and ask yourself a question!

In that split second before your emotions take over, think about what unspoken rule is being broken or what unspoken assumption you are making. With that preconceived notion in mind, ask a question to verify that assumption, such as:

- I'm curious. What result were you hoping for here?

- Can you share what you are trying to accomplish?

- I'm unclear. Would you help me understand your motivation behind this?

- How do you see this helping us get to our goal of _____?

Your delivery of these questions is very important. They could be thrown like a weapon, dripping with sarcasm. The idea here is to ask as dispassionately as possible to prevent blame games from erupting—games in which everyone loses.

Peaches, orange juice, and breaking the rules

Everyone is susceptible to the Fundamental Attribution Error. I learned about a few of my own unspoken rules when our family hosted Alexa, a German exchange student, several years ago.

Shortly after Alexa arrived, I went to the store and bought groceries for the week. Among the things I purchased were eight large peaches and a half-gallon of fresh orange juice. When I got home, I placed the juice in the refrigerator and arranged the peaches in a large bowl on the shelf so my daughter, my wife, Alexa, and I could enjoy them.

Later that day, I found only two peaches remaining in the bowl, a large glass in the sink with orange-juice residue, and the juice container in the trash. I knew that Alexa had been the only person in the kitchen that day. My emotions nearly took over as I told myself quite the story, which went something like this:

"How could Alexa do such a thing? How could she be so rude to take more than her share of the fruit and drink all of the juice without even asking? I had no idea she was so greedy and unkind. What are we doing with a person like this in our house?"

I went from mad to furious as the unanswered questions spiraled in my head. Luckily my wife managed to calm me down before I went to Alexa and booted her out of the house. When I did approach her, I started with, "Alexa, about the fruit and juice..." but stopped when I noticed how emotional she was.

"Chris, I wanted to thank you. My father is a doctor who believes strongly in the importance of having fresh foods in the house. He goes to the store every day and puts out fruit, just like you. He never buys us soda and encourages us to drink all the juice we like. I didn't know that things would be the same so far from home. Thank you for making me feel welcome." And then she smiled and walked off to her room, leaving me stunned and confused.

As I untangled my emotions, I discovered that I had some very deep-seated, unspoken operating rules:

1. One person's ration of fresh food for a week (our typical shopping frequency) is the amount available divided by the people in the house. You may exceed that only if you ask permission of the other people in advance.

2. Juice and fresh fruit are expensive and are not to be consumed at the same time.

We tend to see ourselves doing all we can and other people as flawed.

3. Juice glasses are the smallest glasses available. Tumblers are not to be used for juice.

Without thinking rationally, I had interpreted Alexa's actions as intentional, malevolent violations of my unspoken rules. Essentially, my internal voice said, "The only reason someone would break rules that of course EVERYONE KNOWS would be to hurt me—on purpose! I have to defend myself and those I love against a person like that." Instead, I found out how wrong I was.

Later we had a lively conversation about the difference in family rules and settled on a set that worked for all of us for the duration of her stay.

The reason my stories and yours are usually wrong is that we simply don't have enough information. We can't know the internal drivers, the unseen pressures, the many true stories behind what we get to see. We may believe that we can infer someone's motives from their actions—and the likelihood of us being at least a little off is incredibly high.

Yet if we puncture our own unspoken belief that all the stories we tell ourselves are true, we open up the possibility to explore what's really happening, to get a shared understanding of what is getting in our way, and to work together fully.[22] The ripples of exploring a reality beyond our immediate perceptions and conclusions spread far and wide and can energize other people in a positive and dramatic way.

Exercise 3.3 | **Challenge your stories**

Our internal stories are our default settings—unless we actively challenge them.[23] The trick is that the best time to challenge them is in the moment—right when the story is just about to cause an emotional reaction and physical action. These exercises are to equip you, through reflecting on previous interactions, to prepare you for interactions to come.

1. **Check your track record.** Reflect back on your experience with colleagues and friends. When have you been surprised that your initial impression about a person or situation was wrong? What did you unintentionally miss out on because of a wrong story? What will you do differently next time? Jot a few notes about your reflections in your notebook.

2. **Change one of your stories.** Think about someone you get upset with easily. (If the story's really embedded, you will think of them as upsetting you!) Use a piece of paper and ask yourself what the Crucial Confrontations' authors call the Humanizing Question[24] —"Why would a reasonable, rational, and decent person do that?" Start looking beyond what you experienced to shift the story you are telling yourself, the emotions you are feeling, and the actions you are taking. Write down your thinking and start working to interact differently with that person.

3. **Enlist an ally.** Find a person you trust and ask him to provide you with an alternate point of view for situations you're wrestling with. Ask him to challenge your stories and help you explore what could be happening for the other person. Be open and curious to his perspective, then see how that shifts your interactions with others.

Challenging your own stories is especially hard because they get so deeply embedded and feel so real. The good news is that once you start shifting your perceptions, you begin to see that other people have qualities—often good qualities—you may have overlooked.

LOOK FOR DIAMONDS IN THE DIRT

Practice 3.4 | **Look for diamonds in the dirt**

Helping others see their own strengths allows their greatness to shine.

When you are connected to your own greatness and believe there are more opportunities beyond what you can do yourself, it's a natural next step to seek out excellence in others.

This is fairly easy when people conform to our expectations and stay within our assumptions of what good looks like. Luckily I have had several leaders who looked beyond some less-than-stellar behavior on my part to help surface my real strengths. They didn't judge me as "bad." Instead, they helped me see when my actions weren't helpful, pointed me in a new direction, and encouraged me to use my strengths to help others.

Looking for diamonds in the dirt is seeking out excellence in others, especially when it's not immediately apparent.

Asking a clown to lead the class

I once led a team of civilians and military personnel who maintained a portion of the facilities on an air base. Their mission was thankless and somewhat mundane. When toilets flush, no one notices, yet when they don't flush, it's an emergency.

One young enlisted fellow in our group happened to be something of a class clown. He sought attention by pushing limits and making wisecracks. Unfortunately, he ended up getting a little more supervisory attention than he wanted.

A week after a new regulation prohibiting smoking inside buildings was put in place, I stepped into our maintenance bay and saw this young man, frozen with a lit cigarette in his lips.

This practice is helpful if:

- You are constantly focused on fixing flaws, stomping out failure wherever it starts to show up.

- Employees talk about people's personal and organizational shortfalls—gossip runs rampant to find the next negative focus.

- The organization settles for complacency with language like "Good enough for government work" and "That's just the way it is."

I asked him to report to my office, and when he came in a few minutes later, his posture showed he knew he had crossed the line. He was ready for me to be angry. Instead, I told him how disappointed I was in him. I shared that I could see how he influenced others as a leader, but instead of helping others he was leading them astray. Did he want to continue wasting his potential? He shook his head.

I told him that as a consequence of his infraction, I was assigning him to organize and run our team calisthenics exercise routine for the next month. He was quite surprised.

I explained that I believed he could do a great job leading the group, and then I asked him to get back to work. He headed out the door with a suppressed grin on his face. Virtually overnight his attitude and conduct changed. It was amazing to see the energy and enthusiasm he brought to the program. His teammates and I were begging for mercy as he bounced us through the exercises. By recognizing the latent greatness in him, I was able to help him tap his potential for the good of all.

In the ***Know where you're awesome*** section, we covered how overusing or applying your own strengths without thinking can result in weaknesses in your leadership. This same idea applies to everyone else as well. From the outside it's easy just to see the weakness—the dirt—that is covering up the strength—the diamond—just under the surface. As a leader, your responsibility is to look past the weakness on the surface and help the other person bring out the shine of her strengths. You can also point out if and when you see the person overdoing those strengths or using them without thought, that those strengths are becoming weaknesses.

When clients share frustration about a weakness of another person on their team, I like to ask them, "What's the overdone strength? And how can we harness that strength—in the right amount—to get the results we need?" Their entire perspective can rotate to find possibilities for the person and the leader that weren't there before.

Exercise 3.4 | **Seek untapped greatness**

Where are you seeing dirt rather than diamonds? Since we tend to see what we're looking for, how much are you looking for diamonds in the first place? Here are some exercises to help you shift your thinking and get into a mining-for-strengths mindset.

1. **Do a greatness inventory.** Find a clean sheet of paper and a stretch of uninterrupted time. Write a list of the names of everyone you work with. Remember to include peers and any leaders you follow. Next to each, write down at least one thing that person is great at. For those people where all you can see is dirt, remember that weaknesses are often overdone strengths, and ask yourself what strength may be being overdone.

2. **Shift one thing by getting an outside-in perspective.** Take a few minutes each with three trusted people, and ask them how much they see you seeking success with other people versus avoiding failure. Look for common patterns, and change one of your behaviors to strengthen or shift in the direction of enabling success in others. Hint: choose the most doable change first to get energy to build on your successes.

3. **Boost one other person.** Briefly reflect on people you helped grow past their own limitations or the limitations of the positions they were in. Of the people you work with currently, who seems burdened by their limitations? If possible, use curiosity to explore the situation holding them back. "I've noticed this, and I'm wondering how it's working for you." Support as appropriate.

Since awareness tends to fade over time, it can be helpful to revisit your thinking around these exercises from time to time. Also, if you're keeping a notebook with a page for each person you work with, make sure to note where you see that person's diamond shine, what the dirt may be hiding, and progress as it's made. These are surefire ways to help you see the best in others and start enabling them to grow into their full potential.

HELP THEM FIGURE OUT HOW TO FISH

Practice 3.5 | **Help them figure out how to fish**

Create ownership by asking questions that help others struggle and grow.

You've probably heard the saying, "Give a person a fish and they're fed for a day. Teach a person to fish and they're fed for a lifetime." While this is true, I believe there's a higher calling we can all aspire to around this fishing stuff.

I believe helping people teach themselves to fish can take them even further, and the best way to do this is through asking highly effective questions.

You've probably also heard, "There is no such thing as a dumb question." Unfortunately, I've heard quite a few that didn't strike me as very smart:

- "What the _____ were you thinking?"
- "Why haven't you tried this yet?"
- "Why are you asking me when you should know the answer?"
- "Don't you agree, or is there something you don't understand?"

As a leader, you have the power to ask questions that can provoke self-examination, creative thinking, and problem solving *in the other person!*

One good question can make a difference

An example: one of my CEO clients was struggling with a difficult architect employee who was a brilliant designer yet would frequently lose his temper with staff and clients alike. He both won awards and angered the company's clients. Trying to make a decision about whether

---

This practice is helpful if:

- **You are disappointed that you are the only one who seems to care enough to really understand what the business is about.**

- **Employees aren't thinking for themselves, and are unaware of the implications of their actions and decisions.**

- **The organization seems to learn lessons the hard way, and often requires heroic efforts to resolve problems.**

to keep him or let him go was driving my client crazy. As he shared his frustrations, it was tempting simply to ask, "So why don't you just let him go?" Instead, I thought a moment, remembered a question former CEO Andy Grove used to ask himself, and asked, "If you appointed your replacement, what would that person do?"[25]

Realization spread across his face, and he gave me a knowing look. "That person would fire him and immediately start investing in an effort to find a skilled *and* respectful architect for the business." He sighed. "So even though it's going to be very challenging for me personally, I know now what the business needs me to do. Thanks."

A few months later we'd worked through the change and were wrapping up a meeting when he shared, "You know, the best part about this whole thing is now whenever I get conflicted, I just ask myself what my replacement would do, and it's amazing how much clearer the path becomes in front of me."

It was a privilege helping him figure out how to fish.

Fishing with highly effective questions

Effective questions help others safely embrace the unknown, explore their own biases, be open about possibilities, and resolve their own conflicts, knowing they have your support. Ineffective questions lead others down the path you believe they should take, require them to relive your experience, or reinforce your brilliance and their need to have you around. Effective questions build capacity for the future in the person being asked. Ineffective questions build dependence on the asker.

I've found it helpful to imagine that there is a fixed amount of thinking to be done to answer the question. The less thinking I do, the more the other person needs to do.[26]

To assist you in helping others grow through your questions, here are some tips to help make them highly effective, followed by some examples:

Listen to understand. Suspend your need for having a good answer. This is about exploring their thinking, not validating yours. If you have a thought that you want to explore, jot down a word or two on your notes, refocus on the person, and come back later.

Be curious. Don't make assumptions, and ask questions to uncover the real story. If you do ask a question about an assumption, be transparent and allow wiggle room for the other person to invalidate your assumption. "Based on what I've heard so far, I'm starting to believe [assumption]. Is that the case, or is it something else?"

Follow ambiguity. Where things are cloudy or general, ask for more explanation or detail. If you can notice where you and the other person are *not* going in the conversation because the details are fuzzy, ask about that. You will be richly rewarded because untapped treasure is nearly always on the other side of ambiguity.

Practice positive inquiry. Appreciate where the other person is, and look for the silver lining in each cloud. This is about framing your questions from a perspective that communicates to the other person that she has what it takes to be successful, and that we simply have to find the path to get there.

Help them define success. Find out what really matters to them. One great way to do this is to imagine what would happen without limits: "What would you do if you knew you couldn't fail?" or "If you could wave a magic wand, what would good look like?" This is not a foregone conclusion. Allow for think time, consideration, and interpretation.

Keep the pressure manageable. Imagine having to answer the question you want to ask. Gauge the pressure it creates in you. Squirming a bit is OK, yet if you feel you would have to carefully structure your answer, the pressure is too high. Try rephrasing the question so you get to the same intent of your question without the pressure.

Allow people room to be right. Asking for the *best* or the *most important* thing from someone may seem like it will get to the heart of an issue more quickly. Unfortunately, it often backfires by driving people back into their heads to figure out which of the many answers is most correct. Instead, simply ask for *one* or *some* things that might be important. Most people will then share whatever is top of their mind, which is highly likely to be the most important anyway.

Ask *what* and *how* more than *why* and *yes/no*. Questions that begin with "what" and "how" usually enable people to explore along with you and asserts that their thinking has value. For example, "What do you think a good outcome would be?" or "How do you see this helping us succeed?" In contrast, there is a good chance "why" questions will feel threatening and judgmental to the other person until you have a strong, emotionally positive connection. Consider rephrasing questions that require a "yes" or "no" answer. These questions mean you are doing most of the thinking.

Match the level of the question with the ability of the person. This may sound trite, yet it matters. Ability can be knowledge or understanding, feeling of safety around answering the question, life experience, or simply internal brain wiring that takes time to work.

Stop asking, "What do you need?" and "How can I help?" While both these questions are common for leaders to ask, they are much less helpful than they seem. In essence, you're asking people to be responsible for their own diagnosis as well as their prescription. If they had already correctly diagnosed their own issue, they would likely be working on it, and even if their diagnosis was correct, it's very likely they don't know the best course of action. Instead, try something like, "What's your level of confidence about what to do next?" and follow with "What do you see as your next steps?" to help you both explore together.

Be willing to go out on a limb. If you sense something or find your thinking making a wild leap, call it out, then explore further. This could sound like, "I had a crazy thought just now. How much do you think _____ is a factor here?" or "I'm getting the feeling we're stuck. What do you think?" By calling out what's in your head and following with a question to engage the other person, you both get a chance to step back and find another way to mutually explore the situation. It also shows vulnerability, which can build trust and open up the conversation.

Your conversations may or may not have opportunities to incorporate these suggestions. The key is to be open to the possibilities and to help others figure things out for themselves.

Shift your questions, shift your outcome

These examples illustrate how to help others figure out how to fish.

Instead of...	"Why do you say that?"
Try...	"What are some of the reasons you say that?"
Instead of...	"What is the most important lesson here?"
Try...	"What are some of the important lessons here?"
Instead of...	"What is the problem?"
Try...	"What factors are part of the problem?"
Instead of...	"What do you need from me?"
Try...	"What do you see as your next step?"
Instead of...	"Is _____ happening here?"
Try...	"How much of _____ do you think is happening here?"
Instead of...	"Is _____ important to meet our goal or not?"
Try...	"What parts of _____ do you see as important to meet our goal?"
Instead of...	"Do you think you should _____?"
Try...	"What ideas do you have to move forward?"
Instead of...	"Is it A, B, or C?"
Try...	"Do you think it's A, B, C, or something else?"
Instead of...	"How the heck did you get us here?"
Try...	"How do you think you've done up to now?"
Instead of...	"How are you going to fix this?"
Try...	"How do you see this going?"

Always leave an escape hatch open

Despite your best efforts to ask respectful, manageable questions, you may still overwhelm others. Such discomfort is sometimes unavoidable as you pursue an important issue or explore where people are stuck. So, to minimize the possible negative effects of asking questions, consider making sure there is always a way out. Having an escape hatch means that you structure the question such that it grants the other person permission not to know the answer. This provides the other person a safe environment and allows for more creativity.

My coach, Richard Reardon, constantly builds escape hatches into his questions and comments. Several years ago we were discussing challenges I was having trying to grow revenue in the midst of an economic downturn. Richard asked, "How will you create enough connections to people who need help yet currently don't think they can afford it? I can't think of anything more important for you to focus on." My shoulders were starting to slump as I felt the weight of the question when Richard added, almost with a wink, "Of course, you know if this takes you six, even twelve months to figure out, you'll be so far ahead of your competition they won't even know where to look for you. And you'll have a method that will serve your company through all the downturns to come." I lifted my head, ready to get to work.

Here are a few escape-hatch examples. Say them out loud, and see if you can feel the energy shift inside each statement.

- This is probably one of the most important choices you need to make... and it's OK if you take a month to figure it out.

- Is this A, B, C...or something entirely different?

- Here's how I see your situation... How do you see it differently?

- This is a tremendous challenge...and it's more common than you know.

- How do you want to implement this? Or how much is it even needed?

Just like animals, when we feel cornered we tend to display our worst behavior. If you leave an escape hatch, the cornered feeling goes away. Any pressure that remains can then be converted to get better results.

By the way, leaving an escape hatch open for the other person does the same for you. When there's no requirement for you to ask perfect questions, you can simply shift the questions you do have to give you and the other person a way forward.

Exercise 3.5 | **Move beyond just good questions**

Improving your questions to help others is just one component of deeply respecting others so they want to explore and learn more about what's possible for them. These exercises are meant to complement the material above and move you into action with your team members, peers, and leaders.

1. **Check your track record.** Take a few minutes and list the last five people who've left working with you. Why did they leave? How much did you help them grow past their own limitations or help move them toward their own destinations? Write down your findings and look for any patterns you want to build on or influence.

2. **Raise your awareness of your daily impact.** Take a few minutes and reflect on how much you are prescribing solutions through your questions. Hint: if you're asking people's opinion about an action— e.g. "Don't you think you should..."—it's often a solution in disguise. Another method is to pay attention to the questions you ask others for one day—jot them down for later reflection. Better yet, ask a trusted agent to observe the impact of your questions and then discuss the results with you privately. Again, look for patterns to strengthen or de-emphasize.

3. **Go make a difference.** Choose one person you want to help and spend fifteen minutes connecting with them around the challenges they are having with their work. Listen listen listen. Refrain from solving their problems. (Yes, it's hard!) At the end, ask how this helped them or not, and offer to meet again if that makes sense.

Good questions are a great start to open dialog and empower the other person to really engage. When you engage in practices that encourage deep respectfulness, you may be surprised at the richness that bubbles up in other people. Strong relationships are the best foundation for sharing and multiplying your influence for the benefit of your team, your organization, and ultimately you.

How are you honestly and deeply respecting each other person?

The amount of respect a leader provides determines how available others' strengths are for everyone to use. This next simple assessment can help you see how well you understand yourself in relation to the practices we just covered.

Look at each set of statements and mentally mark an X where you are on the continuum of that practice. Think of this more as a baseline than a report card. And don't cheat yourself—dishonest assessments will not be valuable to you.

Where are you right now on the following practices?

Practice 3.1 | **Trust or have nothing**

I withhold trust until the other person earns it | I begin my relationships trusting the other person | I find others take advantage of my trust

Practice 3.2 | **Mission first. People second. You? Last.**

I take care of my needs first | I take care of others' needs first, then mine | I only take care of others' needs

Practice 3.3 | **Assume most of your stories are wrong**

My stories are always right, so why ask? | I set aside my stories to find out what is real | I ignore warning signs and instead hope for the best

Practice 3.4 | **Look for diamonds in the dirt**

| I wait for people to impress me | I see people's potential for greatness | I believe in people much more than they do |

Practice 3.5 | **Help them figure out how to fish**

| I provide the right answers to help people | I ask questions that explore others' thinking | I'm told people feel their ideas are never good enough |

Consider these questions...

- Which practice stands out as important and urgent for you to address?
- How will working on it help you, others, and the organization?
- What's holding you back from working on it?

RIPPLE | **Self-Assessment:** How are you honestly and deeply respecting...

120

Principle 4

People multiply a leader's power only as much as that power is shared

Principle 1
Leaders' effectiveness is proportional to how well they know themselves

Principle 2
Leaders are judged more by what they don't than by what they do

Principle 3
People discover their best selves through being respected by a leader

Principle 5
Organizations are designed to get the results they are getting

Principle 6
Organizations generating waste are generating opportunities for improve-ment

The success of a leader is determined by how much he or she can positively enable others.

Principle 4

People multiply a leader's power only as much as that power is shared

How you enable each person—as messy and unpredictable as that person may be—will determine the results for yourself, your team, and your organization. This is the fundamental responsibility for you as a leader—helping other people be successful in their roles to ensure the organization can be successful accomplishing its objectives. While not everyone will work out, your failure as a leader to engage others is a direct path to failure for you and the organization.

There are a fair number of people in leadership positions who would scoff at this approach. Whether they prefer to have a competitive, survival-of-the-fittest environment, or just see their authority as something they've earned, these folks tend to focus on preserving their power and authority first. They may be technical experts promoted into the position, and unless you surpass them in technical excellence, they will see you as an obstacle to be overcome rather than a resource and enabler of success. For what it's worth, many of my clients were exactly in this position and were able to shift their approach—and positive results—substantially.

Most people haven't been trained to be leaders, except through on-the-job osmosis. To help everyone, this section connects much of the high-level work we've done up to now in the previous three sections with practical, hands-on methods and recommendations to help leaders help their team members.

Being tightly focused on positively enabling the other person is critical, and at the same time a great strategy can be completely undermined by poor implementation. So here is a fundamental truth to remember throughout your effort of empowering others to optimize their potential:

People respond much better when you do something with them rather than to them.

When you work to empower someone else, what you're really doing is helping that other person discover the leader within him or herself. You're working to help the other person get into *alignment* around personal passion, values, and strengths, and get into *action* around taking risks, being in deliberate motion, persevering, and growing as a person. Since you've already done the same kind work on yourself, you are more able to model self-leadership and tap your experience to share with the person you are leading.

The good news for you as a leader is that it's easier to note the change in energy and excitement, dedication, focus, and flow in others than it is to see it within yourself. Most people can see better outside of themselves than inside, and this gives you a tremendous advantage as you work with the other person.

The not-so-good news is that the same positional advantage makes it very easy to unconsciously impose your own value system and desires onto others. The key is paying attention to where the excitement is. If it's coming from the people you are leading, you are probably helping them find their passion. If it's coming from within you, you may simply be unconsciously using them to meet your own needs.

Where's the excitement coming from, you or the other person?

As a leader, whether you have technical or organizational authority, your enabling actions should be focused on both the short- and long-term success of the other person. This isn't just about getting others to be productive and efficient; it's also about helping them find the path to their long-term success. Ask any great teacher or coach and you'll find that they aren't as interested in trying to make the scores higher as they are in helping their students grow as people who strive to score higher consistently over time.

Ultimately, enabling isn't about making people happy; it's about taking people to challenging places, confronting them with their own abilities and excuses, and pushing them past their current limitations to begin reaching their full potential. If you've ever had a teacher, parent, colleague, or friend nudge you into something and wouldn't let you back down because they saw how much it lit you up, you know what I mean.

"I'll make sure you go down for this..."

Here's a very personal example of how my wife, Diana, positively enabled me through a difficult situation of my own making.

It was my second semester in college, and Diana and I were dating at the time. I had an Aerospace Engineering scholarship through the Air Force that made it economically possible for me to pursue an engineering degree. That semester, I signed up for more classes than I could attend, and as a result decided to drop a physics laboratory class and take it the following semester. I mistakenly believed if I never attended a class it would be automatically dropped.

Imagine my surprise when I got my mid-semester grade slip in the mail with a failing grade! My mind raced. If I failed a class, I would lose my scholarship and be unable to continue in school. In fact, my scholarship contract required me to serve out the rest of my eight-year commitment however the Air Force desired. This was a disaster!

So I did what I had learned to do up to that point in my life. I wish I could say that I went to the physics department, took responsibility for my mistake, and asked for mercy. But I can't. My first response was to resolve the problem while taking as little personal responsibility as possible.

I knew there had been a massive computer glitch in the first few weeks of school that affected many students' records. So I went to the physics department, told them I thought I dropped the class but that it hadn't happened because of the glitch, and asked if they would please update my records.

After listening to my story, the clerk looked me straight in the eye and said, "You're lying, and I'm going to make sure you go down for this." I feigned surprise and left in shock. What now? I was in an even deeper hole, and I fell into despair.

Pouring all this out to Diana, she asked, "Why don't you go to the engineering dean and tell the truth? I know you can do it. No one had ever confronted me that way. After mulling it over, I decided she was right. I met with the dean and shared my story of never attending the class, wanting to drop it, misunderstanding the process, and getting shut down by the physics department. The dean told me he understood mistakes happen, wrote an internal memo to the physics department, and everything went back to the way it was.

Except me. I was forever changed by Diana, who enabled me to rise above my past and to learn for certain how the truth can set one free. She led me through a challenging time by looking for the best within me, and reflected that back to me so I could learn to embrace it as well.

To help you succeed in multiplying your power and that of others, there are four practices in the fourth principle of Ripple Leadership, each building upon the one it follows:

1. **Meet them at eye level.** Starting from where people are enables everyone involved to see what's needed next.

2. **Lead from a half-step ahead**. Staying close yet just ahead of those you lead reduces the pressure on everyone.

3. **Light their torches**. To help others see their own paths, spark the fuel of their personal passions.

4. **Be their outfitter and guide.** Equip others for their own journeys, and tackle constraints they cannot.

So to empower others, you need to challenge, equip, and grow each person you work with, one-on-one.

MEET THEM AT EYE LEVEL

Practice 4.1 | **Meet them at eye level**

Starting from where people are enables everyone involved to see what's needed next.

If you want to positively enable another person, you must meet that person where he or she is. Only by getting as close as possible to that person's current experience will you be able to both empathize with his or her situation and know what guidance will be most helpful.

Remember that as a leader you have a unique, outside perspective the other person does not have. If she had that perspective, she probably would be doing things differently. Your perspective is both loaded with power and likely flawed due to your own unconscious biases, so you must be careful when applying it to the other person.

Many leaders forget to start where the other person is. They place others in a state of insufficiency without even knowing it. They come from an "As leader I know and as follower you don't" perspective that provides the recipient with an unfair choice:

- Submit and feel wrong or stupid, swallow your pride, and try to implement my directive even though you don't feel ownership of it, or

- Rebel (visibly or invisibly) and intentionally do something completely different in an effort to show you are wrong and I am right.

I may be exaggerating. Slightly.

The truth is that meeting a person where she or he is—without prejudgment—provides both of you the best chance to work together toward success.

This practice is helpful if:

- You are irritated that you have to slow down; that others can't keep up with you; that you somehow ended up with the wrong people.

- Employees can't keep up to your standards and are constantly making errors and missing opportunities.

- The organization is constantly slipping deadlines, and you often find out about problems after they are too far-gone to recover from gracefully.

People are doing the best that they can, even if it appears they are not.

Giving someone a real chance to stretch

I once worked with a fellow named David who was part of an IT section that served our twelve-hundred-person organization. He was a little eccentric and prone to sarcastic humor. One evening at his boss' retirement party, after a few beers he sidled up to me and shared that people didn't realize how much power he had. "One little command line and poof!" he snapped his fingers. "Then everyone would really know that I matter." I didn't get too alarmed. I knew that David had been feeling overlooked and underappreciated for some time under his old section chief, and that he was interested in having a bigger role.

My boss, on the other hand, was furious when word got around about David's antics that evening. (Functionally, David reported through his now-gone boss to me and my boss.) "How can he think that threatening to take the organization's network down would be a good idea? There's no way he could run that section!"

"Actually, I think it would be a great idea to support him so we and he could see if he could do it," I said quietly.

After peeling my boss off the ceiling, I asked him to let me have full responsibility for helping David get the best shot possible for the position. Then I shared my plan: David would be appointed as interim section chief for four months; David and I would agree to clear objectives that would indicate success; and David and I would have one-on-one weekly operational meetings and monthly progress checks. David was thrilled, and my boss, somewhat reluctantly, signed off on the plan.

The first few weeks went well, and then a challenge came when one of David's former peers began to misbehave. I coached David through the process, and the situation improved, yet I could tell David hadn't really considered this part of the job. David continued forward, doing a decent job and struggling a bit with the personnel issues. At the last monthly progress meeting, David shared a quiet revelation.

"Chris, I really appreciate you giving me a shot at this. You've supported me completely, and I think I've done a decent job. But I've discovered I don't want the chief position after all. It wasn't quite what I expected, and I have found that I really like what I was doing before." I congratulated David on a great effort, and asked him to use his new experience during the interviews to make sure we got the right person as section chief.

Hearing the news, my boss was nearly gloating: "Told you it wouldn't work." "Oh, I think it worked perfectly," I replied. "If we had held David back and not supported him where he was, his resentment would have just built, and whoever we hired would have had a very hard time with him. By allowing David to try it out with support, he self-selected to stay in his position and support the section. I believe this is a win-win for us and for David." My boss gave me an "I'll have to think about that" look, tipped his head, and gestured for me to leave the office. Over time, the group went on to win awards, and I'm sure David had a part to play in the accomplishments.

Uncover presenting conditions

A confession: I don't know whether it's wiring or conditioning, but my first instinct is to fix things. And if there's not a problem I'm tempted to dig until I find one to have something to fix.

Luckily, years of experience have helped me channel my fixing instinct into doing my best to first understand where the other person is. To really help, I need to suspend my assumptions and judgments and first explore as much territory with the other person as possible. Even as I feel time pressure, I've learned I can either invest time up front or pay dearly over the long haul.

You may possess the same innate instincts. You may want to rush to a solution before really understanding the person. To help you slow down and gain some perspective about the other person, consider these sample questions that will help you to start where someone is:

- Where are you right now personally and professionally?

- Where are you finding success?

- What's holding you back?

- Where are you not enjoying things?

This doesn't mean to take whatever the other person says as gospel. As leader, you have the ability to go beyond the limitations of the other person's perspective and self-reference. Feel free to probe a bit deeper to help him or her and you understand what's happening. And, yes, you may hit up against some personal issues that you can't do anything about except say, "That must be tough." Remember, this is in service of the larger objective of meeting the organizational mission, and while you're meeting her where she is, she has the responsibility to grow and deliver results.

To meet people at eye level, try the following:

- **Stretch yourself personally by putting yourself in his shoes.** If you were him, what might you most want? At the same time, be OK with a completely different form of success than what works for you.

- **Help the other person think of what is possible beyond the current conditions and limitations.** As you progress working with her, requests rather than orders usually inspire more ownership by the other person.

- **Help him feel validated.** Be sure to acknowledge how he is feeling and what he's dealing with.

- **Take a risk with the other person**. This isn't "here's how I did it so you should too." Instead, allow yourself to be vulnerable about the uncertainty in your path and empathize with her situation. This will enable her to feel safe exploring her own vulnerability.

- **Do not tell him what to feel.** Instead, tell him what you feel and what you are going to do, and that will provide them with an excellent example to do the same. If you do this well, he will rise to your expectations to the limit of his abilities.

When you meet people where they are, everyone gets a stronger foundation upon which to build and grow.

Exercise 4.1 | **Meet others where they are**

Understanding where each person is starting from is a vital first step to helping that person grow. These exercises reveal where people are and help them develop in ways that help you, them, and the organization.

1. **Turn on your tractor beam.** Find out more about one of the people you work with. Invite her out for a 15-minute break. A way to start is asking what got her interested in her career field. Ask some or all of the questions listed above in the *Uncover presenting conditions* subsection. Be ready to answer any question you ask her. When you're done, write down the important points in your notebook to help remember them. The following week, invest another 15 minutes in a different person.

2. **Seek dissatisfaction.** It's counterintuitive to actually look for dirt instead of diamonds. Yet people who are irritated, slightly on edge, or pushing back are often those who care the most about what needs to get done. Invite one of these people for a 15-minute break. Once there, set some healthy limits upfront to prevent a gripe session. Let her know that you wish you had more time yet you do have fifteen minutes. You noticed she seemed to want to do more than she was being allowed, and ask if she would be willing to give you a high-level overview of what she wants to make happen and what's holding her back. Then, listen, listen, listen.

If you meet people where they are, you give them the best chance to succeed in their personal situations. And that will help people around you know that you're there to help them grow and contribute, no matter where they're starting from.

LEAD FROM A

HALF-STEP
AHEAD

Practice 4.2 | **Lead from a half-step ahead**

Staying close yet just ahead of those you lead reduces the pressure on everyone.

I have a special responsibility when I work with others to release their full potential: I go first into the unknown. To help create an environment of success for the other person and myself, I need to be a half-step, and only a half-step, ahead of him or her. Mentally, emotionally, and physically.

Not thousands of feet ahead, yelling instructions from above to pull harder on a long and lonely rope, like some leaders today who are too busy strategizing to listen to their staff. Not sitting in a warm basecamp miles down the mountain, radioing in encouragement, like some leaders today who stage pep-rally meetings yet don't know what motivates their people. I'm right there, shoulder-to-shoulder, yet ever-so-slightly ahead of the person I am leading.

This idea of the half-step has helped many of my clients take a tremendous amount of pressure off themselves. They no longer feel the anxiety of being the perfect leader, selecting the perfect course, doing everything far in advance of when it's needed. Instead, by being themselves and connecting with others, they unconsciously give themselves permission to learn through doing in their development toward being an excellent leader.

I've heard some people say that leadership is a contact sport. It's easy to be in contact with your followers if you're just a half-step ahead. You can glance over your shoulder to make sure they are able to keep up, and they don't have to yell to provide feedback or encourage you to keep going. When they're close, you create a loop of energy that serves everyone.

This practice is helpful if:

- **You find yourself trying to figure out or guess where the team really is, then scramble to adjust.**

- **Employees hesitate, appearing not to know what to do next, or they are just doing whatever they want with little connection to what's really needed.**

- **The organization doesn't go anywhere while you're away or not involved. You have to be there to push. Or you feel you have no influence and bad things are happening that you can't seem to get in front of.**

Leading through vulnerability, just a half-step ahead

Our company does a lot of goal-focused teambuilding with senior leadership teams. These projects last about three months and involve the team in an intense, multi-day offsite plus follow-up check-ins at 30, 60, and 90 days. Throughout this time, we work with the team leader to help him or her be a half-step ahead of the team and the process.

One particular leader had stepped into a newly formed team and was, frankly, quite a mess. The CEO had promoted him ahead of his bosses. While this leader was an excellent candidate, the political situation made for challenges on top of the already difficult technical issues and market conditions the company was facing.

I facilitated the intensive, three-day offsite. The team and leader did great collaborative work together, setting a goal for the next 12 months, understanding their top priorities, strengthening relationships, and committing to each other to make it happen.

Later, during our debrief at the end of the offsite, I sensed something was missing for the leader. Rather than worry I had left something out, I shared the struggles I had personally from being a leader of a team with challenges. I wasn't looking to guide this leader directly—an "I did this so you should do it, too"—but instead was simply reflecting on my experience so we could both examine it for connections and potential helpful information.

At one point in the conversation, I decided to be very vulnerable. I pointed out a strength I wasn't sure this leader was aware of. I went out on a limb and shared that during the offsite he was very in tune with what was happening, and even seemed to be operating on intuition. I shared my own personal experience of being an engineer, being taught that objective data was all that mattered. And I also shared that as I started leading others over time, I became aware of my intuition. It almost frightened me that I somehow instantly knew things I had no way to know objectively. For a while I fought my intuitive ability. But I slowly learned to trust it. And when I did, I found it to be tremendously helpful in leading others.

Sharing those personal insights triggered a turning point. Opening up about my own experience around intuition significantly deepened our discussion. In response to my transparency, this leader started reflecting out loud about experiences in his past and seeing the possibility of his having and using intuition, which he also had previously discredited. By seeing a possibility within him and sharing my own experience, together we began to consciously tap an ability he could use to lead himself and his team in more profound ways.

I didn't have to teach him all about intuition or declare myself an intuitive master or ask him if he thought he was intuitive. I simply related the experiences I had that connected with some of the ways I saw him working as a leader, and his awareness of his own abilities expanded.

It's possible I could have been wrong. If so, he probably would have listened politely to my brief story and thought it interesting yet irrelevant. And we would've pressed on.

Yet if I had waited for him to discover for himself how to be consciously aware of his intuition and how to use it, he and I would have missed out on a lot of opportunities for his organization to benefit from his heightened awareness.

Some people who coach leaders believe they already have the answer. Others believe the client has the answer. I believe in something in between—working together, leading slightly, yet staying close. This is what I mean by being just a half-step ahead.

What this means for you

Staying a half-step ahead is both liberating and challenging. There's no magic formula for the distance that best serves leaders and followers. Instead, here are some practical guidelines to help you find and maintain the space that helps followers trust the leader and provide feedback while also allowing the leader to move forward without losing connection with followers. If you pay attention to these parameters and trust your team, you should be able to stay connected and a half-step ahead:

You *don't* need to be a complete expert in everything the people you lead are doing. In fact, many organizations who promote technical experts into leadership positions often find they end up producing super-contributors who inhibit the growth of followers through micromanagement instead of effective leaders who grow people past their own capabilities.

It's more about them than it's about you

I don't look for clients to leap up in the middle of a discussion, smack their forehead, and say, "Damn, Chris, I can see that I've been coming at this completely wrong for the last nine years. Your insights have enabled me to realize what I should be doing and what an idiot I've been. You are brilliant, and I couldn't have done it without you!"

I'd rather have them experience an *aha!* that bounces around in their skulls: "Oh, now I get it. From this new perspective, the thing I've been struggling with is clearer and now I can let it go. This helps me both understand what's really happening and get into different action to resolve it."

When we see those quiet, internal shifts—we call them "private epiphanies" at our firm—that actually lead to better external results, we know that all the hard work we've done together has been worth it.

You *do* need to know enough about the process and business fundamentals to—as I call it—throw the BS flag. You need to know what's most important and what's noise, when processes are doing all they can and when they could be better, and when to ask questions to help people explore and understand the big picture. Partner with other people to learn, yet make sure their limitations don't become your own.

You *must* be willing to learn—especially challenging your own assumptions. Make your points like you know they are right, and listen like you know you are wrong. Without humility you'll soon find yourself leading no one.

You *must* point out things the other person can't see—and that includes things that might be painful. Most everyone is in heads-down mode, getting work done. If you've ever had an accident where someone later tells you they could see it coming and figured you did too, you'll know the reason for this one.

You *must* communicate effectively and regularly. Being a half-step ahead is like having someone draft you when you're bicycling. The other person gets a tremendous advantage being so close to you because you're blunting the wind resistance, yet if you turn or brake quickly without first communicating to the other person, you can almost instantly create an accident that tangles you both up.

You *do* need to be both tough *and* fair. You're demanding excellence from yourself and others, yet you're also providing honest, specific encouragement and helping other people grow both their abilities and their faith in themselves.

These tips can help you find the place where you are both stepping out and staying connected with those you lead. Being willing to be vulnerable and seeing your role as serving the team from slightly out in front will help you be a Ripple Leader people choose to follow.

Exercise 4.2 | **Set the pace a half-step ahead**

Stepping out the right amount for your team and your organization to succeed can be a delicate balancing act. You need to pull the team forward, yet you need to be close enough to them to stay connected with them. These simple exercise steps can help you ensure you're at the right pace for your team and you to succeed together.

1. **Check your stride.** Ask three trusted people where they feel you are on the spectrum, from way behind, to alongside, to way ahead of the team. Make sure to tell them you are seeking a fully truthful answer. Adjust your stride as needed.

2. **Shift from pulling to encouraging.** Honestly answer the question: what would happen in the first day / week / month if you had to leave suddenly? Validate with a trusted source to find out how much you're pulling the team and organization. Shift the energy you were using to pull to helping others step forward. You'll know you're on the right track if your sudden departure would slow yet not stall the organization.

3. **Map out what being a half-step ahead would mean with different people.** Position a piece of paper horizontally and make four columns. Label the left-most column "Person," the second "Now," the third "A Half-Step Ahead," and the last "Awesome." In the left column, list people whom you would like to help. Next where they are now, then go to the last column and imagine where they could end up. Then come back and think of the next small half-step that could help them move toward Awesome. For example:

Person	Now	½ step	Awesome
Sue	Low trust from mistake	Trust of peers	Trust of entire org.
Ken	Making his numbers	1 Stretch Project	Home runs!
Lori	Overloading herself	Delegate 1 task	Sustainable performance

Ask yourself questions around what's next for them to uncover. Think how you might be able to lead them from just slightly ahead of where they are. Doing this on a regular basis, say, quarterly, will go a long way to helping people stretch themselves toward greater success.

As you set out on a heading with your team close by, it is critically important to stay connected to what's happening with the team. Understanding their strengths and passions can help you make sure they are accessing the fuel and light that all of you need to go as far as possible together.

LIGHT
THEIR
TORCHES

Practice 4.3 | **Light their torches**

To help others see their own paths, spark the fuel of their personal passions.

Many leaders believe that the light cast by their beliefs and passions is enough to inspire their team. My experience has taught me that for any team to achieve its potential, each person's beliefs and passions have to be as bright and clear as possible. Without people who believe in themselves, appreciate their own strengths, and are tapping into their own passions, there is no one to lead and leadership doesn't matter.

Unfortunately many people settle for what they have, becoming complacent with the everyday rhythms of work and home. As fear creeps around the edge of their lives, their response is to pull well inside the circle of known safety. This is the default setting that keeps our species surviving, yet not thriving.

As a leader, you have a singular advantage to overcome the default setting of others—your perspective. Your position allows you to see both the possibilities and the default, scarcity-driven behavior of people. If you are willing and able, you can reflect your perspective back to people and help them see their strengths, feel their passions, and seize their opportunities.

Sometimes the light is under cover

When I was manufacturing microchips, I had the good fortune of being on the same team as Blayne.

Blayne worked in the wafer manufacturing plant as a technician. His appearance was unconventional: he wore black t-shirts from heavy-metal

This practice is helpful if:

- You spend time with people then find your strength drained and theirs recharged. It's almost like you are other people's battery.

- Employees seem to be dragging at work, going through the motions without any real interest, and very little commitment to anything beyond the bare minimum.

- The organization seems to be on a very slow treadmill.

bands and sported a few eyebrow and other piercings long before body jewelry was acceptable. Based on his appearance, it would have been easy to dismiss him as someone who wasn't serious. And many people allowed themselves to be swayed by how Blayne looked instead of finding out what he was capable of.

One day when we were meeting, I asked Blayne what he wanted to do. He started describing his daily tasks when I stopped him and asked him again what he wanted to do—with his career. He looked a bit shocked and said no one else had ever asked him that at work. We talked together for a while, and he opened up. He wanted to be an engineer. He loved to code computer programs. I knew he had a drive for excellence, and I pledged that I would do what I could to help him achieve his dreams.

At that time, our factory was merging with another on the campus, and I asked for Blayne's help in doing testing and qualification of the multimillion dollar process machines I was responsible for. The results we got with Blayne's help made the other engineers envious. Thanks to Blayne working his tail off, our machines were qualified long before most other sections. I believe Blayne was able to better tap his strengths and desires because I helped open the door for a deeper connection to them for both of us.

As I write this, Blayne is a lead software engineer. Had I not looked beneath the surface with Blayne, I would have lost the opportunity to get his excellent help, and perhaps he would have not have given himself permission to achieve his dreams.

Accessing the best in other people requires paying attention to what they do best

To light another person's torch, there are three things you must bring together for them: passion, vision, and strengths. These items are essentially the same components you strengthened as part of the first principle of Ripple Leadership: **Understand what matters most, Chart your own course**, and **Know where you're awesome.**

Understand what matters most...to each person

Just as I mentioned in the Self-Leadership practice of ***Understand what matters most***, everyone has their own personal navigation gauge that can guide them toward their own deep passion and interest. However, most people underplay their strengths and haven't yet thought explicitly about the values that are important to them.

Luckily, in your position as a leader you have a unique vantage point to notice and point out where the "signal strength" of other people's passion is strongest. When a person is connecting to their passion, you'll see physical indicators:

- Eyes brighten and widen
- Vocal pace and inflection increases
- Gestures grow more fluid and animated
- Expressions become more genuine and spontaneous

Often helping another person can be as simple as pointing out where you see the indicators go up, and asking what about that activity is important. Over time the other person will be more conscious about what's most important to him, allowing you both to understand his values better. With this understanding, you can collaborate with the other person to create a role that leverages those values.

Help them chart their own course

As with you and your personal goals, it's important to enable the other person to figure out what she wants and commit to it herself. Without commitment and the right reason, at some point the person you're serving (and yes, Ripple Leaders are primarily a servant to others) will realize that she is living someone else's dream and not her own—and what happens next becomes highly unpredictable for everyone!

It can be amazingly helpful to bring the other person's future back to today, ask challenging questions, listen, then probe for fit and commitment. Just be careful that you're not trying to convince him or otherwise validate the future you would like for him. If you feel the need to push a bit, be transparent: "If I could choose, I'd pick this future for you because of [valid reasons connecting to their passion]. I'm curious...what do you want to do and how does that fit for you?" Feel free to stretch the person beyond his comfort zone. Just be sure it's in the direction *he* wants to go.

Some of my clients have been hesitant to focus on what works for their employees, fearful that the company will lose when people realize their future may be outside it. I've countered that with, "Wouldn't you rather know now that this person won't be here long term and begin planning or working toward a smooth transition?" Also, I've seen multiple instances where listened-to employees have become much more productive and focused, even in cases when they realized they would probably leave the company sometime in the future. When team members see the leader working to create an environment where everyone can succeed, they can't help but feel a part of something special.

A good place to start is with the mission and vision of your organization. Asking something like, "If our organization succeeded living out our values and accomplishing our stated mission and vision, what would that look like to you? And what role would you have played?" can create a safe place for you and your employee to explore the future together.

Once you're on the same page, then you can shift to each employee's overarching purpose: "If we're completely successful, what does that mean for you? How does that add to your own personal mission?"

When you're both in a place of shared respect and purpose, communication will flow and you'll be in a great position to co-create a pathway toward mutual success that leverages the other person's strengths.

Help them know where they are awesome

You can use the same techniques of observation to note where people excel—and don't be surprised if they deny having strengths!

As I shared earlier in ***Know where you are awesome***, when I point out my clients' strengths, they're often dismissive, saying, "That's just what you have to do" and "Everyone does that." You'll face the same challenge helping others realize that often a strength is something they believe is easy. I usually raise their awareness by asking how often other people disappoint them around that strength. Nearly always the response is a slightly puzzled look and, "You know, now that you mention it, it's strange to me why some people struggle with something so easy." That's when you can help them understand that's a strength for them!

Just as third-party assessments can be helpful to you personally, they are also an excellent way to get common information for the people you're serving and for you to look at together. When the assessments reveal information that you both agree is accurate, it will be easy for the other person to absorb and use. Information that runs contrary to their self-understanding yet matches yours, on the other hand, should be jointly explored...and then given time to soak in with them. After all, the only way for the information to ultimately help is for them to personally embrace it as helpful.

Make sure to foster ownership

While many leaders guess the situation facing others and then consider what they personally would most want in that situation (the Golden Rule), it's most effective to involve the other person from the get-go and ask her what would work best for her (the Platinum Rule).

Remember to ask good questions, as we covered in ***Help them figure out how to fish***. While "What do you need from me?" or "How can I help?" seem straightforward and clear, these questions often put too much pressure on the other person. It's essentially asking him to simultaneously diagnose his challenge, prescribe a solution, and determine what you can offer as part of that solution. Occasionally you'll work with someone who knows all these things off the top of his head. But more often, you'll need to explore each piece with him.

Again, most employees will find it more helpful if you ask questions that help her explore her thinking and experience:

- What will be important for you to have in this situation?

- How have you dealt with situations like this before?

- What worked best?

- How will you know you're on the right track?

As you explore possible solutions, be sure to pay attention to his stress level. There's a fine line between positive struggle that will result in a great solution and negative overwhelm that will cause withdrawal and failure.

Let her know that she doesn't need a perfect solution, and also resist the temptation to solve the problem for her. Remind yourself that a less-than-ideal solution created and owned by her is far better than a perfect solution designed by you.

Exercise 4.3 | **Strike a spark**

These exercises will help both you and your employees plug into their hopes, values, and strengths. Using them regularly will not only help you help them, but the practices will also begin to take root in their own leadership skills so that they can help other people grow.

1. **Ask your top three people what would make their heart sing!** Explore with them where they would most like to go. This is more about the qualities of the future rather than actual work positions. A lower-pressure alternative is to ask people what their latest obsession is, i.e., what they focus on besides work. Then watch where they light up.

2. **Write down where you see the potential of each person on your team.** Start looking for evidence where that is happening today and reinforce it. You will be surprised at how much untapped potential is available—and so will the people on your team.

3. **Write down the passions of your top three to five employees.** Stumped? Most leaders are—at first. Hint: what do they invest their time in, perhaps when they're not at work? It's amazing to me how often I get blank stares from leaders when I ask them what motivates each of their people, their peers, and their own leader. Take a few minutes and a clean sheet of paper and note what you see people get interested in and enthusiastic about.

4. **Give an earnest compliment to three different people each day.** Point out the specific behavior, why this behavior is important to your company's success, you, and them. You'll know you're really making a difference when you see people emulating this pay-it-forward behavior and doing the same.

Knowing what we're best at, what matters, and where we ultimately want to go is critical preparation for the journey we need to take together. The next step is to help equip and outfit everyone for the journey.

BE THEIR OUTFITTER AND GUIDE

Practice 4.4 | **Be their outfitter and guide**

Equip others for their own journeys and tackle constraints they cannot.

If you want to hike through wilderness or climb a mountain, you would be smart to hire a guide and outfitter.

Guides know the terrain, the weather, and the routes that will keep you safe and help you arrive at your destination. Outfitters understand what equipment can accelerate your progress and what can hinder it, and what would work within your experience level or what could overwhelm you.

And really outstanding guides and outfitters understand the most important critical success factor in every great experience—that the experience is yours.

Outstanding guides ask questions about what you want out of the experience. Why are you going? What do you personally desire from getting to the destination?

Outstanding outfitters ask questions about what you'd like to learn to do or try on the trip. How much do you want to work versus enjoy the ride? What have you always wanted to do that this experience can provide?

Then these professionals use their experience to anticipate the obstacles and challenges that might await you and them. What could get in the way? How could we prevent the problems before they occur? How can we make this experience the best possible?

Armed with information, these guides and outfitters marshal support by helping supply whatever you don't have—equipment, expertise, manpower, resources, you name it—that you will need to overcome any obstacle and have a successful experience.

This practice is helpful if:

- You wonder why people aren't getting things done—people constantly come back to you for everything.

- Others complain they can't do their jobs or they settle for the way things are with a fatalistic attitude: "We've got what we've got, so live with it."

- Organizational focus is on keeping people equal versus tapping individual strengths for the good of the whole.

In a similar way, Ripple Leaders equip and guide their people to achieve the mission by anticipating challenges and bridging the gap between what's available and what's needed.

Knocking down barriers versus lauding authority

I was fortunate to have an outstanding leader, Colonel Thomas F Wilson, during one of my Air Force assignments. He asked me to go help a group of civilians whose mission was to manage and make available resources of funds, personnel positions, real estate, and computers to a 1200+ person organization. Unfortunately, this group had misinterpreted their purpose and saw themselves as protectors of the resources instead of providing them to the people who needed them to do the work.

"Whatever it takes, Chris," Colonel Wilson told me. "I'm empowering you to do whatever you need to do to eliminate barriers to success for this group and our organization."

"Thanks, Colonel," I replied. "Your support means a lot since I may have to be a bit unconventional to succeed." He raised an eyebrow, yet shook my hand and wished me luck. The previous civilian division chief had just retired, so I was assigned as deputy to the new civilian division chief.

For the first few months, rumors flew that I was the Colonel's henchman, there to eliminate positions and fire people. Instead I listened respectfully, supported anyone who took a small risk, and went out of my way to recognize excellence whenever I saw it. Through my consistent behavior, I managed to earn the trust of a few people who filled me in on the negative culture created by the previous boss, dominant even after his departure. I become even more focused on both people and the mission, and I continued to seek win-win outcomes.

Working late one evening, I heard a quiet knock at the door. "Come in!" I answered loudly. An employee named Mike opened the door, a bit reluctantly. "Please, sit down," I invited.

Mike sat on the edge of the chair near my desk and we talked for a bit, then he stood up to leave. "By the way, I thought you should know there could be a problem with..." He mumbled something I couldn't understand and started moving toward the door.

"Mike, I'm interested. Would you please tell me more about this? I'm curious—fill me in."

After a lot of listening and a bit of prodding I asked Mike what he would do to solve the problem. "Are you kidding? Me? I don't have the authority to solve this problem," Mike protested.

"Humor me," I gently insisted. Mike eventually gave me three options, which I asked him to narrow down to one. With reluctance, he did.

"I have a proposal for you, Mike. Let's say you put this solution into place. If it goes well, I will tell everyone that it was your idea and I simply supported your implementation of it. If it goes badly, I will tell everyone that it was my idea, and despite your implementation efforts, it didn't work."

Mike sat quietly for a few moments, then said, "So there's no way I can lose on this?"

Following the success of Mike's project, I began to have a series of knock-and-talk conversations in my office with different people who just needed a little support taking barriers down to achieve the success they deserved.

A few months later and after a series of wins, Colonel Wilson was happy to recognize the fine work this division was doing to enable the rest of the organization. While I was proud of my role, I was even more proud of the people who rose above their challenging history and succeeded together at a higher level.

It's a long journey, and no one does it alone

Of course, the real results always come from the people involved in the journey—yet those results will be limited or enabled by the leader's ability to guide and equip each person on the team. This is where you pull everything together for the people you lead, and here are the five tactics you'll need to be successful:

1. Ask effective open-ended questions

As we covered in *Help them figure out how to fish* earlier, effective, open-ended questions are powerful tools to build engagement and commitment. Here, those questions can help jointly define the outcome of the program, project, or role. A few to get you started:

- What does success in this program/project/role look like to you?

- What difference will that make to you and others?

- How important is this to you?

Open-ended questions can also help people get unstuck. But watch out. While it feels rewarding to "fix" things for others, resist the urge. There is significant value in helping people work through a problem themselves because it can give them the confidence and ability to tackle the next problem when it comes up. At the same time, don't abandon people to struggle and fail needlessly. It's a tough call to make as a leader, and you'll likely fail a few times yourself before you can really *Lead from a half-step ahead* effectively. When you're not sure, I recommend giving the other person more responsibility rather than less. People often have untapped reserves that can surprise both you and them. So to help a person who's stuck get a little perspective, try questions like:

- What will you do next?

- How does this issue make you feel about the future?

- How does this issue make you feel about the progress you've already made?

- What does this challenge say about you and this journey?

Make sure you *Meet them at eye level* and *Light their torches* by pointing out their best qualities as well as where the other person is in alignment around their own vision, strengths, and values.

2. Rally resources and knock down barriers

As Mike's story shows, people usually put their heads down and just do their jobs when the problems facing them are beyond their capability to tackle. These situations can only be changed by a leader who helps people and teams successfully rise above current limitations to a better future. Even as you step in to help, make sure you are enabling as much of the other person as possible, asking questions like:

- Who do we know who would know how to succeed?

- What resources do we have that we haven't even tapped yet?

- Who do we know who could connect us to someone who would know? What professional and online networks could we ask?

Share your own knowledge and experience, yet strive to offer it as a comparison point and not as "The Answer." Help the other person mine your knowledge for information needed to unlock the solution, but make sure she is holding the key.

Also make sure to provide and not artificially withhold real-world resources, such as funds, overtime, tools, outside training, coaches, etc. I can't tell you how many times I've been in meetings where multiple people worked for hours trying to work around a problem that could have been expeditiously solved by purchasing something that cost less than a hundred dollars. It's more often than not a strength gone bad. In the spirit of doing more with less, teams often unconsciously overconstrain themselves. Being lean and creative is one thing; starvation and suffering is quite another. Remember the Goldilocks curve and aim for that just-right amount of proactive and responsive resource support, no matter how much or little the person you're working with can do.

3. Augment with meaning

When my middle daughter, Rebecca, showed me an accomplishment from school that she was really proud of, I could have told her how great it was and how much I liked it. Luckily the experience of others before me helped me shift my reaction from praising to probing. I asked her questions like:

- How does that make you feel?
- What do you think made the difference?
- How much do you want to do more of this?

You should have seen her light up! It was fun for both of us, and by helping her examine her contribution and how it tied to what's important to her, I believe her win was all the more powerful.

Providing context for the greater purpose of succeeding in the current project or issue is one of the most underused tools in a leader's toolbox. A great way to do this is with earnest praise. Share the specific results, the specific behavior that made a difference, and how the results specifically impacted you, the team, and the organization. The ripples from these compliments can go very far indeed.

And you don't have to wait until the project is done. When you see people working hard, you can stop and interrupt. Let them know that what they're doing—right now—is what separates those who get to do what they love from those who have to go to work. Those people may look like they are the same, yet the people doing what they love to do will enjoy it, get higher productivity, and last far longer than the people who show up and just tolerate their jobs."

Augmenting with meaning can make the difference between laying bricks and building a cathedral—especially when you have to step back and redo some of the wall.

4. Examine results for lessons learned

Good, bad, or ugly, it's often the leader's responsibility to help people figure out what really happened, what was expected or surprising, and what can be done the same or differently next time.

When I work with leaders on communication, sometimes we video-record the person speaking and then watch the recordings together. I know from personal experience it can be painful to see yourself making mistakes, yet the process of watching is critical to understand what went well and what can get better. We watch for trends and patterns in the speaking to enable the leader to understand and take control of their speaking. Only when you compare actual results to what you were really seeking can you adjust and improve.

I once worked with a professional writer who was struggling to make her business successful. She was great at collecting information, and we soon discovered that the difference between the profit she earned working on work she was passionate about versus the amount she made on uninspiring bulk work was a factor of three times. We coined the term "profit density," and by aiming to increase it she dramatically reshaped her business to provide her greater satisfaction and profitability while allowing her more free time to do what she wanted.

5. Celebrate privately and publicly

I had a boss who would always celebrate milestones privately first with individuals before deciding on whether to do a public celebration. Often the other person was pleased that the accomplishment was known only to colleagues and the manager. Perhaps the person being recognized didn't want to appear to be gloating to his colleagues, or perhaps he wanted to keep things quiet in case the successful milestone didn't fully pan out. Either way, rather than requiring a public celebration, this boss always met people right where they were.

Sometimes the boss just wrote a short personal note—a small, private celebration. Other times he would help the person realize how the public celebration of a victory would boost camaraderie and spirit, sharing how important it is to be part of a winning team. He taught me that while a celebration may seem hokey, most people chart their progress by memorable low and high points with organizations. As a leader, he took on the job of making it easy for everyone to remember the high points. And because of that I try to follow his example.

By guiding others you can help them see more clearly where they're heading. By exploring with them what they might need on the journey, and getting them the help they need, you ensure their success, your own, and that of the organization. It's that simple.

Exercise 4.4 | Guide and equip people for the journey

People can and should do a lot of work on their own, and yet your involvement can make the difference between senseless struggle and hard-won satisfaction. These exercises are built to get you started finding out where you can make a difference helping to guide others and remove barriers from their path.

1. **Listen and empower.** Take a few minutes and connect with someone on your team. Ask, "What drives you crazy about your job?" Listen carefully and be curious, not defensive. Then ask, "How would you change it?" Take a few more minutes and brainstorm ways it could happen. Then sort the options by doability and impact, and support the person to try one.

2. **Look where others are struggling.** Take a few minutes and write a list of your organization's projects. Reflect on where we're not making progress. Take some more time and ask where the challenges are. For example, how are we doing with direction, resources, and skills? Apply guidance, equipment, or organizational clout as needed to get the project unstuck.

3. **Check your ownership of other people's problems.** Take a few minutes and mentally catalog the unfinished work around you—paper, electronic, and projects. If you were suddenly able to do only half as much, what would you decide not to do? Start guiding and equipping others to reduce your level of involvement. Get assistance from a trusted agent if needed to start helping others help themselves more.

4. **Write down what success would look like for each person on your team three to five years out.** If you get stumped, be curious about how they got into what they do and look for the passion and interest. Project that interest forward. Where does it lead? Explore this with them. Bonus points depend on their level of engagement. You may have to overcome lack of momentum or stagnation.

You've just finished learning about and practicing better interpersonal leadership. The stones you just skipped will continue further into the organization, spreading positive ripples as they go. Next up are the policies, processes, and methods that need your help and the help of your people so your organization can run effectively and efficiently.

How are you positively enabling each person to succeed?

Your willingness and ability to remove barriers for others—and sometimes even yourself—determines how much their strengths can be harnessed for everyone's benefit. This simple assessment can help you see how well you understand yourself in relation to the practices we just covered.

Look at each set of statements and mentally mark an X where you are on the continuum of that practice. Think of this more as a baseline than a report card. And don't cheat yourself. Dishonest assessments are not valuable to you.

Where are you right now on the following practices?

Practice 4.1 | **Meet them at eye level**

I expect people to meet me where I am	I meet each person where he or she is	I start with everyone like they don't know anything

Practice 4.2 | **Lead from a half-step ahead**

The people I lead don't influence my pace	I strive to stay just slightly ahead of everyone	I maintain distance between myself and my people

Practice 4.3 | **Light their torches**

I set equally high expectations for everyone I work with	I work to tap the strengths and passions of everyone	People decide how they want to show up

Practice 4.4 | **Be their outfitter and guide**

| Sink or swim— it's up to them | I provide resources and encourage with real feedback | I can smother people with "help" |

Consider these questions...

- Which practice stands out as important and urgent for you to address?
- How will working on it help you, others, and the organization?
- What's holding you back from working on it?

RIPPLE | Important points about leading other(s)

Important points about leading other(s)

Reflection and repetition allow us to learn lessons from what we've already heard, read, and done. Here's a summary of the important points from the section on Leading Other(s):

Principle 3

People discover their best selves through being respected by a leader.

Trust or have nothing

Like oil in an engine, trust makes everything run well. Without it, you get friction and struggle.

Mission first. People second. You? Last

You need to be able to put others' need before yours.

Assume most of your stories are wrong

Prejudging another's intentions limits both of you more than you realize.

Look for diamonds in the dirt

Helping others see their own strengths allows their greatness to shine.

Help them figure out how to fish

Create ownership by asking questions that help others struggle and grow.

Principle 4

People multiply leaders' power only as much as that power is shared.

Meet them at eye level

Starting from where people are enables everyone involved to see what's needed next.

Lead from a half-step ahead

Staying close yet just ahead of those you lead reduces the pressure on everyone.

Light their torches

To help others see their own paths, spark the fuel of their personal passions.

Be their outfitter and guide

Equip others for their own journeys and tackle constraints they cannot.

CREATE RIPPLES BY LEADING

THE ORGANIZATION

Many leaders believe the best place to start effecting positive change is working on the organization. It's often easiest to see the problems "out there"—mistakes from departments not working together, processes that are holding people back, and results that don't meet goals.

Unfortunately, as companies get bigger, they tend to create too much structure. They get caught in the illusion of a system being able to create results without people. It's like throwing a stone out as far as possible instead of trying to skip it. Kerplunk! This can suck the spirit and energy right out of people who work there, especially those who feel value in getting things done. There's real danger in trying to fix an organization by policies and procedures alone.

The truth is, while an organization will not achieve greatness without a supportive structure, structure alone cannot make the organization great. To realize lasting success, an organization has to be well-designed, well-run, and enjoyable for the people who work there.

The best path to get to the successful organization is first to set up and prepare to release the stone. Strengthen your ability to lead yourself, and practice the right tools to apply yourself effectively to building structure that works for you. Next, release the stone to respectfully involve and engage others to improve themselves and their results. If you've done this all with the right approach, the stone will skip out to the organization so everyone can collectively help the organization and its systems achieve sustainable success.

When an organization is designed, built, and run well, it helps everyone understand how to contribute, push in the same direction, and enable achievement no one could produce individually. Correctly made and

> Structure significantly influences behavior, thereby dramatically impacting results.

maintained, an organization holds everything together by fostering positive interactions among all its components in an overarching effective and efficient system.

In this next chapter, the two principles in Leadership of the Organization are:

Principle 5—Organizations are designed to get the results they are getting. The design of every organization determines the results it gets. Want different results? Design differently.

Principle 6—Organizations generating waste are generating opportunities for improvement. Run and refine the organization to minimize waste and maximize output.

Leading the Organization is after Leading Yourself and Leading Other(s) because it builds on our human need to be connected to something bigger than ourselves. When a group of people is aligned in purpose, able to work together, and using everyone's individual strengths, they can achieve nearly anything they set out to do. Structure—the organization—is the container of pooled resources and enabling rules and standards that make it possible to succeed and improve together.

Understanding the most important principles at play within your organization allows you as Ripple Leader to help your team successfully leverage those principles. And applying yourself to the following practices can do just that.

Principle 5

Organizations are designed to get the results they are getting

Principle 1
Leaders' effectiveness is proportional to how well they know themselves

Principle 2
Leaders are judged more by what they don't than by what they do

Principle 3:
People discover their best selves through being respected by a leader

Principle 4
People multiply a leader's power only as much as that power is shared

Principle 6
Organizations generating waste are generating opportunities for improve-ment

Want different results? Design a different organization.

Principle 5
Organizations are designed to get the results they are getting

Many leaders are keenly focused on efficiency—driving waste to zero, maximizing profit per hour, or otherwise making sure that every bit of effort is moving the organization toward the goal. This mindset is helpful for organizational leadership. But it can also be a burden. The problem is that leaders with this focus are frequently ahead of themselves. Instead of marching blindly toward efficiency gains, the first and most important questions they should be asking themselves are "Are we aiming the right direction? Are our goals the right goals? Are we doing the right things to get there?"

When the answer to all those questions is "Yes!" for your entire organization, it is designed for effectiveness. And that means "Yes!" for the result of the overall organization, not just for each component. Optimizing individual parts of an organization usually results in a suboptimized organization overall. And to optimize the entire organization, it's virtually required that much of the organization be running in a suboptimized way.

A widening gap between desired ends and reality

While working as a process engineer, I got direct experience about how important organizational focus on effectiveness can be. Our organization supplied companies with microcontrollers that did everything from activate air bags to run kidney dialysis machines—important stuff. The machines that made these devices were very complicated and had to be operated properly or the devices would fail testing or worse, fail in the field—with potentially disastrous consequences.

The instructions—"specs"—to run the machines were written by senior-level engineers, and over time all the things NOT to do were tacked onto the end of each document. Engineering carefully controlled these specs because ultimately the instructions should have determined product quality. However, these instructions were virtually unintelligible to normal humans, including our operations and training departments. In desperation to help people understand and follow the right processes, these departments wrote training documents for operator training and certification.

Ever so slowly what the specs stated and what people actually did on the floor diverged. Changes the engineers made to the specs sometimes got into the training documents, sometimes not. Only when we were challenged by some of our customers on low product quality did we discover this silent and unconscious conspiracy to create an ineffective result for all. In the end, through some steady prodding by senior leadership, the engineers and trainers got together with the best operators and wrote one set of operating and certifying instructions into each spec. Confusion was reduced, process consistency improved, quality went up, and customers were happier. Our organizational effectiveness soared.

To design your organization for effectiveness, there are four practices in the fifth principle of Ripple Leadership:

1. *Use everyone's crayon in the picture.* When people see their influence in a shared future, they become owners.

2. *Know what's in the black box.* Understanding your organization's systems is the first step to using them well.

3. *Work backward from the outcome.* Start with where you want to end up, then trace back each preceding step to today.

4. *Make the right things easy.* Helping people do the right thing by default makes life better for everyone.

Each of these practices focuses on a different aspect of the organization's design, and together they can enable you and the people you lead to create a highly effective organization. The most important of all of these is establishing a clear, shared picture of what success looks like.

Practice 5.1 | **Use everyone's crayon in the picture**

When people see their influence in a shared vision of the future, they become owners.

There. I've said it. The vision thing.

As leaders, we seem to have a love-hate relationship with vision. On one hand, we know it can be a critical element to get everyone's effort aligned. On the other, we tend to produce vision statements that don't excite or help direct people's best efforts.

Out of a desire not to leave people out, we end up with meaningless mush or an operational organization chart—neither of which inspires anyone.

So where does this internal conflict around vision come from?

Some of it comes from all the time we spend thinking about big picture strategy. Our brains are working on the vision 24/7, and we're completely sick of the vision when everyone else is just starting to get it.

Some of it also comes from the language we use to describe these grand ideas. Is it our vision? Our purpose? High-level strategy? Our mission?

Bottom line: As long as the picture of the future is shared and helps everyone in the organization understand where we are trying to go—together—it *doesn't matter what we call it*. It's simply the future brought back to today so we can use this understanding to make better decisions, now. Our vision of the future needs to be clear and understandable enough to function as a litmus test for all decisions. Do we help this client or walk away? Is this opportunity inside or outside of our strategy? How much do we need to innovate versus not rock the boat?

This practice is helpful if:

- You have a clear picture of where the organization and people could go, yet no one seems inspired or interested. It's like pushing sand up a rope.

- Employees compete to come out on top with other sections or people, especially by withholding information and helpful effort.

- The organization has pockets of excellence, yet at times is working at cross-purposes.

A shared picture of the future can make the difference between the grudging compliance of slapping bricks on a wall and the enlightened engagement of crafting a cathedral one brick at a time.

I'm definitely not advocating vision-by-committee, the mushy stuff so bland and uninspiring that it diffuses any joint effort of substance. I'm advocating for involving the people who count in the creation and adoption of the vision so everyone owns it. And for making sure that everyone is moving in the same direction.

To be fair, many organizations do develop a mission / vision / purpose statement, and some do it very well. The best statements enable people to see themselves and their actions compared to a clear, desirable end state that they believe is achievable.

Most of the rest of the statements are usually either dictated by the senior leader or assembled by committee with the positive intention of providing a guiding light to the organization. Unfortunately these statements are overstuffed with hidden meanings or the language is so vague that they do not fulfill their purpose. Instead, they allow everyone in the organization to believe that the picture of the future in his or her head is the same as their colleagues — which generates further problems when everyone in the organization needs to be working towards the same goal.

So in which direction do we need to go?

Imagine if your organization was on a boat, with everyone having their own oar. It's almost certain that no one would be pulling in the exact same direction. Why? Because everyone has a picture in their own mind of the end goal — and those mental pictures aren't the same. The more people and the bigger the boat, the worse the problem.

Because of this, many people in organizations are pulling against each other. The sales team pulls toward their ideal future of massive revenue, while the engineers pull toward technical excellence, customer service pulls toward wherever the customer needs help, and the operations folks pull toward maximum throughput. People get tired of seeing the other group heading "the wrong way" and taking actions that are not helping go "the right way"—their way. In some organizations I've even seen people row so hard in different directions that the boat breaks apart and sinks.

All we need is someone to ask "Hey, what if we all rowed the same direction?" Not a precise compass heading, but roughly in one direction. Sure, some people would row a little left and a little right of that heading. Yet with a component of everyone's rowing going the same direction we'd suddenly have wind in our faces and a wake behind the boat. People would feel like they were doing something—together—that actually made a difference instead of churning up foam, getting tired, and ticking each other off. People might even start sharing the load and swapping sides of the boat to keep each other's arms fresh.

To help you see what I've just described in another way, here is a simple visual model and story we've developed through our work with clients. We call it the **Bubble Diagram**:[27]

In the beginning, someone had an idea. This person saw a set of possibilities, a new way, an achievement worth going after. And it was good.

Other people were attracted to the idea. Some saw the value of a subset of the idea, and were excited to help make that happen. Others had related ideas that connected with the original idea. An organization formed with diverse ideas and people. And it was good.

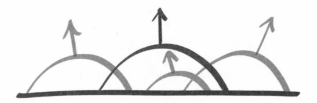

Everyone labored hard in the direction they believed the organization was going. However when different results began to occur, people began to get irritated. In their minds (and sometimes out loud) they wondered, "Why is that other person doing those things? That won't get us to where we're supposed to be going!" And the other people they were speaking about wondered the exact same thing about them. Groups of people within the organization began to clump together around the methods they thought were "right"—in other words, headed toward the destination they believed was correct. Silos began forming around different groups in the business. Conflict around the "right thing to do" began to get heated. And it was not so good.

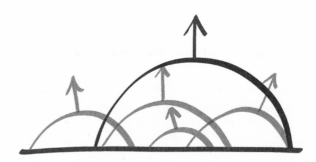

The conflict grew until someone asked out loud: "Where do we want to go...together?" People began to see that until everyone agreed to an overall outcome, all the different ideas and methods were causing problems rather than creating better solutions. So everyone sat down and jointly committed to a set of outcomes that would require the diversity and hard work of all to achieve. A few people realized that the future they personally wanted to create was not what the

organization was committed to, and decided or were asked to leave to
create that future somewhere else. And it was much better.

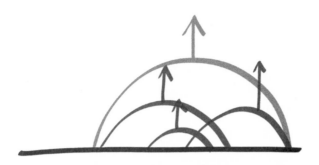

Everyone began to work much more effectively together.
The different ideas and methods brought to the organization resulted
in vigorous debates and rapid experimentation—and the organization
moved forward quickly by building on everyone's best ideas and methods.
Eventually the organization attracted other new and better ideas and people
that fit within the shared direction—and everyone provided their best for
the benefit of all. And it was very good indeed.

Color a complete picture

When you involve those who will actually build the future in the creation of the picture first, you significantly increase the completeness of the picture, especially around things you may not have thought about. And you will also substantially increase the motivation of others to make the shared picture a reality.

Some leaders scoff at setting a joint direction, saying the team's job is to follow the leader's direction, and that the leader is responsible for the vision. Steve Jobs had this perspective, and saw his role as chief decision-maker and direction-setter. He was very successful in setting a singular direction for Apple—up to the point where he wasn't around to enforce that direction. I believe the future success of Apple lies in the how people who remain can create a joint picture of the future as powerful as what Steve might have envisioned.

As you co-create the future, it is important to consider the qualities and values so the picture of the future is easily understood and embraced by everyone.

I once worked with a company whose leaders came up with a picture of the future that was presented as, roughly, "world domination by the end of the decade." While clear and brief, it did not help people discern how to get there. Would it be ok to cheat a client? Beyond a market leadership position, what did world domination involve? Was it just the lucky survivors who would emerge victorious? The picture did not have enough clarity for anyone to use their judgment beyond doing what would gain market share.

Great pictures enable people to have a shared sense of the qualities of that end state. These shared aspirations enable everyone's actions to move the organization in the right direction, so the end state pulls everyone forward like a magnet. And those pictures have embedded within them the values for which the organization stands.

Great visions also have values embedded in them as lenses through which everyone can look to understand what behaviors are acceptable and not acceptable in attaining that vision. What success looks like is very dependent on how much that success is valued by you and the team— according to your shared values.

Ideally, every written or drawn picture of the future is simply evidence that collective thinking and understanding has taken place.

Exercise 5.1 | **Picture a shared future...together**

These exercise steps build on each other. Getting clarity for yourself and others about the future is a messy, imprecise process that will pay tremendous dividends to everyone involved even if the picture ends up a bit blurry. In other words, picturing a shared future is one of the best ways to involve people in creating an organization and goals they see as their own.

1. **Do some structured dreaming about what you want the business to look like in the future.** Take a blank piece of paper and 15 minutes to think about how you want the company to succeed. A good format is the Achieve-Avoid-Preserve method in the *Chart your own course* section. This step is critical to enable you to create a simple framework that you can feel confident allowing other people to build on.

2. **Get other people's perspectives on what the future could look be.** Ask five different people to spend a few minutes with you on what they perceive success for the company to look like three to five years into the future. Listen listen listen. When done, compare their unique pictures of the future to yours and find the common connections.

3. **Allow others to sketch out their parts of the picture.** Put elements of your picture on the wall—the messier the better to invite people to improve upon it—and leave it up for a few weeks. Hang a marker pen nearby with some sticky notes, and encourage people to make notes on it. If you've done a sufficient job getting the most important points covered, additions by others will augment and not hijack your vision of the future.

Taking the time to build a shared future is critical since it enables everyone move past deciding where we are going and then to focus on how we are going to get there together. The next step is to make sure you fully understand the organization—the system—that will take us to that future.

KNOW WHAT'S IN

THE

BLACK

BOX

Practice 5.2 | **Know what's in the black box**

An understanding of your organization's parts and connections is requred to help everything work together.

To use a car to get you, people, and equipment from point A to point B, you don't have to understand its systems. You simply get in, turn the key, and drive to where you want to go.

However, if you want to optimize your use of the car to get the best possible combination of gas mileage, safety, speed, and comfort, then you need to fully understand how the technical and human systems work and interact. You make sure the tire pressure is correct for the load you're carrying, the windshield is clean, and everyone is wearing their seat belts before you set out on a trip.

Sadly, most business leaders get in their organization every day, turn the key, and drive off without checking the oil or really thinking about how the organization operates—until it begins to run a bit rough. And often running rough means that damage has already occurred. It's like throwing rocks at the pond without paying attention to where they're landing.

The recent near-death of the US auto industry could be attributed to this attitude. Many leaders seemed not to understand the moving parts in their industry—especially the shifting attitudes of American car buyers. As the need for increased gas mileage and quality impacted sales, many manufacturers kept tossing stones that didn't skip out to positively affect their customers. They focused on the needs of their business internally first, and eventually the lack of success with customers was one of the major factors that required them to get help from the US government and taxpayers.

This practice is helpful if:

- You are constantly working problems yet feel like you're just putting on Band-Aids.

- Employees put the results of their section or function ahead of the organization.

- The organization tends to approach every problem as completely unique.

While you may not be able to tune your business every minute of every day, understanding how it works as a system can help you run and tweak it better. There are a variety of ways to achieve such understanding. My mentor Richard Reardon introduced me to a particularly good way to systematically think about organizational systems that has proven very useful to my clients and me.

How's your system working?

Richard's diamond model begins with the organization's vision and goals illustrated at the top of the diamond. This is where the organization wants to be in the future.

The bottom of the diamond includes the organization's people—the combination of skills and abilities, motivation and inspiration, and thinking and doing that enables the vision and goals to be achieved.

The sides represent the structure that connects the vision and the people.

On the right are roles and standards. These enable the vision to be broken down into doable portions, while also clearly setting expectations for results and behavior from the people.

On the left is a system of management and feedback. These feedback systems compare desired results with what actually happened. This information flows back to people, who then use this information to adjust their efforts and how they fulfill their roles to enable the organization to get closer to the desired vision.

Many company leaders think they are done after they set out a vision and get some good people in place. Unfortunately, without roles and standards, the people will perform poorly because they lack the system and expectations needed to work effectively. Without management and feedback there is little information and support to get better. Frankly, without all the components, it's a recipe for disaster. The good news is that making a ripple here is as easy as sketching a picture. You can use this model to assess if you have all four pieces well defined. If not, that's a good place to start.

Another way to look at your black box

Another way to understand your organization is to make a system diagram. Here's a simplified system diagram for my company, Trebuchet Group:

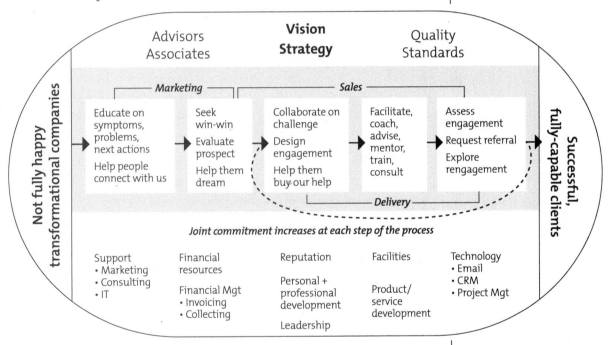

Our overall process is geared to the outcome of clients who are more successful and capable. The more our clients are pleased with the results we have helped them achieve, the more likely they are to refer us to others. These are the most important ripples we're aiming for collectively as a company, with subsequent skips that occur when we do it right.

This system diagram allows us to see what it looks like when our efforts are on-track and working together, and also lets us know which dials and knobs we can adjust to continue to keep the quality of our results high. A simple system diagram can be useful for showing customers or training new team members. It can also help you to periodically review your process flow to make sure you are focusing on the most value-added activities.

On the left are our ideal clients—companies who want to positively transform their community, industry, and world, yet who are having challenges doing so.

At the center is our primary process of attracting and helping clients. You may notice that Sales starts as part of our Marketing early on and continues even during Delivery. We define sales as all the work to create and improve our relationship with our clients.

Above the process are the most important assets and direction for our company. At the bottom of the graphic are the supportive systems and resources we tap to help our clients.

If all goes as designed, we take prospective clients through the process, which equips them to be fully functional and able to achieve their goals. Afterward, they provide referrals to other companies who could use our help.

Understanding the systems and how people fit into them is critical to improving leader and team decision-making. I once had a great illustration of both while serving in the Air Force.

Getting into hot water

During my military career, I led a section that had the responsibility to maintain the dormitories on an Air Force base. Many of the junior enlisted personnel were housed there and really didn't have an option of living elsewhere. Unit commanders were very sensitive to any problems in the dorms since those directly impacted morale.

During a spell of unseasonably warm weather, my commander called me to share that the other commanders were complaining about the dorms being too warm. He asked me to have my team switch to cooling earlier than normal that year. So I went to the crew responsible and got quite an earful.

The chief explained to me that the temperature control equipment was a centralized, one-pipe system—meaning that we could only put hot or cold water through the pipes into the radiators in each dorm room. The problem was that changing between heating and cooling operations literally took the better part of a week to re-pipe the system connections from the boiler to the chiller. He predicted we would triple the workload if we changed too early because chances were that we would have to re-pipe to heat and then re-pipe back again to cool before the spring was over.

Armed with this new information, I met with my commander and informed him of the details of the system. "Thanks, Chris," he told me, "but I'm betting we'll just have change once and the reason we're here is to support the mission of the other units. Please switch the system over."

Back to my team to explain the commander's rationale and decision, and despite some grumbling a crew left to go execute the order.

A few weeks later the weather indeed turned frosty again and at my commander's staff meeting he turned to me, apologized, and asked me to have my team change the system to heat again. In turn, I met with my chief, apologized for the extra work, and gave the order to change back to heating.

Later that afternoon I got a call from the commander, saying he'd already heard that the rooms were warmer and complimenting us on the rapid turnaround. As I hung up, I heard snickering in the break room, and noticed the crew was already back. I went to the chief in his office, and when I asked what was up I got a wide grin.

"Well, you see, we didn't exactly change the system to cool—a few weeks ago we just turned off the heat. It took us just a few minutes to turn the heat back on," he said, smiling. It was clear he felt he had pulled a fast one on the commanders. Yet his smile didn't last long when I shared my perspective on the situation.

"I could be angry at you for not doing what I requested, but I have to say I'm mostly disappointed. I'm disappointed because you and I have just trained our boss on two things that won't help any of us in the future.

First, anytime he wants something done and I tell him how long it will take, he's going to mentally discount it by 80% and tell me that he knows my team—your team—can get it done much faster." The chief's face fell. "Second, we've just taught him that the system is far simpler than it really is. He now thinks any change just takes a couple hours. I think we just signed your crew up for lots of challenging work in the future." Needless to say, the chief was not happy about this.

The main point here is that leaders need to know how the system works to be able to make effective decisions about changing the system or adjusting its operations. I did fess up to my commander that we had developed a new possibility between cool and heat—the nothing option. We had a good laugh and moved on.

Exercise 5.2 | **Think of your business as a system**

This exercise is meant to help you reinforce your understanding of the components of your organization and how they work together. It should help take some of the knowledge you're using implicitly and pull it out of your head so you and others can explicitly understand it to be able to make it better.

1. **Sketch out your diamond.** Draw the diamond model on a piece of paper. Add in appropriate details to the corners. Once your system is defined, you can use this model to troubleshoot problems. The solution to a challenge in any area will usually come from adjusting the two connecting corners.

2. **Draft your own system diagram.** Get a clean piece of paper and sketch a system diagram for your organization. Think of this as a bad draft to get your internal critic to take a coffee break!

    a. Stay simple and sketch out the big pieces. Start on the left side with the input— your prospective clients. Draw your primary process in a few steps from left to right. If there are lots of variations feel free to flowchart them out at a high level—don't get stuck in the weeds!

    b. Put your primary assets and direction on top, and your primary support and resources on the bottom.

    c. Describe the output of your process on the right side.

    d. Keep handy and tweak as needed so you know where to focus and adjust your organizational system

3. **Get input and support from others.** Using either diagram, ask people who know your business (employees, managers, key suppliers, even clients) to contribute. Find out what's missing or what you've assumed away.

Many leaders get stuck working in the tactical day-to-day and are unable to see the big picture. Now that you have a simplified understanding of your organizational system as a whole, you can improve the system step-by-step by starting at the outcome and working on the steps and methods required to achieve it.

WORK BACKWARD FROM THE OUTCOME

FINISH

START

Practice 5.3 | **Work backward from the outcome**

Start with where you want to end up, then trace back each preceding step to today.

It's easy to get caught up in the more-better-faster culture that surrounds us. If you're not early, you're late. If you're not busy, you're lazy. Push, push, push.

When we push, we get things moving yet constantly have to shift which way we're pushing to keep things moving in the direction we want. In contrast, when we pull we create movement automatically in the direction we're heading. If you've ever tried pushing a heavy suitcase (versus pulling it along) you know what I mean.

And yet mentally moving to the end result and pulling from there is very difficult when our day-to-day lives demand forward progress on whatever is next on our to-do list.

Urgency clutters up our inboxes and desks and can take on a life of its own. It's very easy to become lost in doing things just to do them, disconnected from what's most important and why we're doing them.

It's hard to find the important stones we should be skipping on the water when a sand-like stream of very small things is constantly covering them up. That's why effective leaders are constantly digging for what's most important—figuring out the outcome needed before taking action.

Intentional outcomes, or just results from activity being done?

Stephen Covey famously taught people to be more effective by being outcome-focused, to "begin with the end in mind." One way to get to

This practice is helpful if:

- You are not sure what levers to pull to get the results you need.

- Employees focus solely on getting their function to look good and meet their goals, despite other functions' needs.

- The organization is busy yet not producing the results needed.

the outcome is to ask yourself or others, "Let's pretend this activity is done—what does that result look like? What do we get?" Keep asking those questions until you get to something that sounds like a real outcome instead of just a step in the process. If we don't know what the desired impact is, we may just be going through the motions.

This practice connects to both **Be their outfitter and guide** in helping equip people for success with a clear destination, and with **Use everyone's crayon in the picture** by ensuring shared understanding of the qualities of the desired end state. All three practices work together to help everyone aim at the outcome, own it, and take steps to get there.

Working our way out of this challenge requires a different mindset about where to start.

Cheating by starting at the end

Pencil-on-paper maze puzzles are my favorite example of pull-vs-push relationships. I discovered early on in my childhood that the best way to do these is to start at the end and come back to the beginning. It's much easier to see the path this way because you encounter far fewer dead ends.

While some people might call this cheating, virtually all of the most effective production systems work using the same idea. Toyota created the kanban system[28] in the 1950s to send signals about customer demand back down the production line, ensuring production made only what was needed. The Theory of Constraints,[29] developed by Eli Goldratt in the 1980s, further refined techniques to optimize workflow and process to minimize overall waste and delay in a production system. These are just a few examples of systems that stem from the premise of starting at the desired result and working backward to get the most streamlined and effective results.

The key is to be clear and comprehensive about the results you most desire. As Lewis Carroll said:

If you don't know where you are going,
any road will get you there

Objectives need to be objective

The "we'll know it when we see it" objectives organizations have are understandable. We're often dealing with something we've never dealt with before, and if we have seen it we aren't certain that we can achieve it again. In start-up mode, these kinds of objectives may be tolerable as the organization starts to define itself. Yet if left undeveloped, they are totally insufficient.

Great objectives include the following information:

- What is the outcome? What does it look like? How will we know when we get there?

- When will it be achieved? What's the timeframe for the objective?

- Which single person is responsible? Who's involved?

- How often does this objective have to be reached? How much sprint versus marathon?

Simple, yet not simpler

I like to paraphrase Oliver Wendell Holmes Jr when I say "Simplicity on this side of complexity is worthless. Simplicity on the other side of complexity is priceless." In this context, this means picking a few measurements simply because they are easy to measure is not helpful. Yet distilling complex processes down to the few measurements that are most indicative of success has tremendous value.

Whenever I see or hear an organization elevating one measurement above all others, I get nervous. Remember ***More is not always better***? I once spoke with a company leader who shared privately that his goal was for his company to pay no taxes ever, and that he was investing tremendous time and energy to be able to achieve this goal within five years. He was shocked when I told him he was underselling himself—I was certain he could achieve his goal by the end of that month. He looked at me expectantly, and I'm not sure how happy he was when I shared that the quickest path to his goal was to shutter his company!

Multiple measures can prevent suboptimization

People are extremely creative and can suboptimize any system to maximize whatever results you want, but at what cost? There are always tradeoffs and tension between outcomes—happy staff vs high levels of profit, throughput vs quality, speed-to-market vs feature set—and the best organizations measure and find methods that simultaneously increase outcomes that are otherwise in tension. Instead of the tyranny of the **Or** (as in "We can do this **Or** that"), these companies seek the genius of **And** (as in "We can do this **And** that").[30]

Ideally the critical few measurements you choose should represent both a short- and long-term focus. For instance if you want to be successful driving a car, you will have better results if you pay attention to happenings in the near-term (like the speed of traffic ahead of you) and long-term (how often the engine oil is changed). Here's an example from a client:

For most companies, positive cash flow and profitability each quarter are their end goals. New Belgium Brewing Company in Fort Collins sets its goals out a bit further by incorporating two other elements of a triple bottom line—impact on people and the planet. They approach projects and business looking for an improved community and staff as well as lowered production costs, reduced waste, and a positive environmental impact.

With the mindset that waste from one process could be fuel for another, they have done everything from using waste heat from the brewing process to preheat process water to building a co-generation plant at the brewery to use methane gas (another waste byproduct) to generate electricity. By setting their goals with a holistic perspective, they are able to achieve results that are good for everyone involved.

How far you go really does depend on where you draw the finish line. By designing with the desired end state first—orders fulfilled, products built, customers happy with results—you significantly increase the odds of getting to that end state while simultaneously preventing wasted materials and effort.

Exercise 5.3 | **Improve your ability to work backward**

The following exercises are simple, short ways to examine and improve your ability to design goals and plans that start from the outcome and step back toward today. Using this approach you can ensure the path to your desired goals is as effective as possible.

1. **Do a quick review of your company goals.** Grab your most current goal sheet and critically examine each goal. How much pull is there versus how much push? How intentional are the outcomes versus just an extension of what we do today? How holistic are your measurements of success versus how much are they focused on a single aspect of what you believe your company is all about?

2. **Take a challenge and figure out the desired outcomes.** Pick something difficult and ask a few others "What do you think the end goal is? If we all got to do the right thing, what's the final result?" Compare answers and look for overlaps to uncover shared understanding (or lack thereof).

3. **Build a bridge to shared outcomes.** Building on from the step above, take that same problem—along with the shared understanding—to people and ask "What comes right before we get there? What do we need to have to make that happen?" Keep asking until you can trace back to what to the next steps that you and others need to take to move directly toward the desired destination.

4. **Review and adjust reward systems.** It's tragically common how often functional goals and rewards are set up—mostly unintentionally—in ways that pit people and sections against each other rather than encourage people to work together. Do a quick review of your systems and ask "How much do we have conflicting or zero-sum rewards?" Then do your best to modify the systems to have collective rewards, even if there are goals that conflict with each other. Reward optimization of the whole instead of optimization of individual or functional goals.

With clear, comprehensive, and shared outcomes to focus on, the next step is to smooth the path of the organization in that direction so the right things are the easiest things to do.

MAKE THE
RIGHT
THINGS
EASY

Practice 5.4 | **Make the right things easy**

Create systems that get the best result by default, and make the worst result hard to achieve.

The path of least resistance is a physical phenomenon you can use to shape your business to run well by default. The ripples that come back to you and other people from using this practice provide energy not just the first time, but every time you undertake the activity.

Removing barriers and increasing flow

When I was a kid, I would go out after the big summer rainstorms and play in the gutters at the side of the street. The rainwater would pool up behind my dam of sticks until it was easier to go around, over, or through the dam. Water always follows the path of least resistance.

People also act as forces of nature, naturally seeking the path requiring the least amount of effort.

A classic example of this is how one college determined where to put paths across an open area on campus. They simply seeded the entire area with grass, waited a few weeks, and then paved the paths people had made. The more worn the path, the wider the sidewalk.

Where the college didn't want people to walk, it didn't put up a little "Please don't walk on the grass" sign. Instead, it added a few spiky bushes and a small fence. People could have climbed over. But they didn't. Why? Because they took the path of least resistance—walking around the obstacles to the shortest path that led to their destination.

Surprisingly, many business processes make it very hard for employees to do the right thing, while at the same time allowing conditions where it is

This practice is helpful if:

- You find yourself cutting corners because the right things take too long.

- Employees take the low road—even worse, people are kept when they violate standards yet get results.

- The organization is making mistakes that in hindsight were very preventable, and procedure exceptions are the norm easy to do the wrong thing. Such businesses might say, "Well, we hire good people who do the right thing because they know the difference between right and easy." Sure, and how much more could those same people accomplish if they didn't have to work hard to do the right thing?

It's nearly epidemic how often people end up working around barriers instead of being empowered to change them.

Reduce friction where you want speed and throughput

When an organization's or team's velocity needs to be accelerated, reduce the friction that's preventing them from accomplishing the things they need to make happen.

Think of a simple, intuitive, and easy path of execution.

It can be as simple as the way my dad took care of the problem of having to figure out the right ratio of oil and gas for the chainsaw. He taught me to write the proper ratio of oil and gasoline on both my plastic fuel container for my chain saw and on the saw itself. A few pen marks make it easy to quickly know the right amount of oil needed without having to go find the manual. Even better, I found oil bottles that have just the right amount of oil to create the right ratio when mixed into a full container of gas.

And it can be as involved as putting up buildings faster than anyone thought possible.

Faster than fast

A few years ago I worked with a precast concrete company in a very competitive market. The company bid a job that would require their crews to erect panels at nearly twice the rate they had ever put up panels before—yet the company leadership felt they needed to get the work. After winning the contract, the slightly-shocked leaders and foreman of the erection crew got together to figure out how they could deliver the results needed.

The crew was shocked because they had been working for a couple years to improve their speed by 20% - and the new requirement was 100% faster. After some resistance and grumbling, they began looking at all the places where they could possibly compress time. First, they looked at which roles were the bottlenecks, where others always seemed to be waiting for them to finish. The welder's time was one constraint—multiple welders wouldn't be practical, yet they could have other people do prep work to maximize the time the welder was actually welding. Up to that point, no one did anyone else's job.

A second area the team looked at was non-value-added time spent on site. They pointed out that the connecting parts and tools used during assembly showed up at the jobsite mixed in boxes, so a lot of time was wasted trying to find the right part. The team again crossed a boundary, this time around the role of the crew loading the materials back at the plant. The loading crew even agreed to the extra work of prestaging the materials in reverse order in the boxes so the last thing in the box was the first thing that needed to be used on site.

I spoke to the team leader after the changes had been in place for a week. He almost jumped through the phone, nearly incredulous: "Up to now, our previous record was 12 panels in a day. This week we've done over 25 panels a day and the team believes we can still get better. Even the old crusty guys who were fighting the changes are enthusiastic!" He paused for a second, then said, "At the same time, I almost feel bad about it."

When I asked why, he shared, "If this capacity has been there the whole time, have we been letting people down by not realizing it sooner?" I assured him that, up to now, he and his team always did the best they could.

The company ended up having to start work in different areas around the site because they got so far ahead of the other contractors. Making the right thing easy for the welder and the crew created a new normal of amazing possibilities they hadn't even dreamed of before.

Where is your organization inadvertently preventing people from doing their best work by requiring them to hurdle barriers that don't add value?

Make the right things the easiest to do, and the wrong things the hardest.

Add friction where you want to prevent things from happening

Some barriers are good, like those inserted to deter bad behaviors or ineffective ways of working. Unlike reducing friction to make things easier, here we want to do the opposite—increase friction to make it more difficult to do things we don't want.

Most businesses have some sort of delegated financial authority to prevent fraud or mistakes that would cost the business money. Yet the most effective barriers are those where you as a leader channel organizational energy in the right direction.

During my Air Force career, I served under then-Major Carlos Cruz-Gonzalez. He was responsible for operations and maintenance of the facilities and grounds of an Air Force base with a few hundred civilians and military personnel under his command.

Part of his role was formally recognizing excellence, recommending promotions, and otherwise ensuring morale was good. One day during a staff meeting he shared that he was seeing a disturbing trend.

"I've been noticing that while I constantly have requests for high ratings of our personnel, there are few if any submissions to the Airman and Civilian of the Quarter award programs." He looked around the room and waited. People began to fidget, not wanting to say that filling out the form each quarter was seen as less important than other tasks.

"Some of you might think I will withhold recommendations for promotion until I get better quarterly award submissions. I would never do that as it would hurt our service members and civilians." Yet the collective sigh of relief stopped short as Cruz continued.

"However, I believe it's critical that we create an environment of excellence here. If you are unable to submit award nominations, I understand - and I will expect instead a three-page report detailing the situation and your corrective action plan to help your people be able to be recognized as excellent. I will hold you accountable for the plan you create. After all, our unit and our people deserve nothing less."

The next morning a stack of award nominations awaited him on his desk.

Another form of adding beneficial friction is mistake-proofing. Ideally this is where the wrong action is physically impossible to make.

In the United States, leaded gasoline is no longer available. However there was a time when you could get leaded gasoline, unleaded gasoline, and diesel fuel at the same filling station. To prevent engine and catalytic converter damage, unleaded gas nozzles were made a smaller diameter than leaded gas nozzles, and both were smaller than diesel nozzles. Vehicles had correspondingly sized filler holes to prevent someone putting diesel into a gasoline powered car, or leaded gas into an unleaded gas engine. (Diesel engines are a bit tougher and some can take a tank of gasoline, yet the system requires diesel owners to do their own checking for the right fuel.)

In most organizations, it is hard to make it *physically* impossible to do something. If there's a way to do something wrong—regardless of the jigs and safeguards and penalties—people will find a way to do it. Humans are darn creative when it comes to going around a system to get the result they want. So the next best solution is a combination of structure and peer pressure to comply with the structure.

Doctors at first saw simple surgery checklists as an insulting waste of time, yet many are beginning to embrace them as they have proven highly successful in preventing missed steps in critical procedures. In some cases, the team cannot proceed unless everyone agrees. While many surgeons complained checklists were unprofessional, in *The Checklist Manifesto* author Atul Gawande documented they reduced complications and deaths by 35%.[31]

In summary, designing organizations around paths of least resistance is about making the right action the easiest action. When you promote execution along paths of least resistance, you help individuals and teams focus energy on the result instead of on what they have to overcome to get there.

Exercise 5.4 | **Put friction where you want it**

Like a pair of ice skates that allow you to glide smoothly across an ice rink, the ideal situation reduces resistance in the direction you want to travel, and increases resistance in the direction you don't want to go (sideways!). This exercise explores how to harness both aspects of friction to benefit your organization.

1. **Find out where others are being driven crazy.** Take a few minutes and ask your key people what's holding them back: "What drives you crazy about your job? What do you wish you could change? What have you resigned yourself to doing in your work?" Then partner up with them to change the system and reduce friction so it's easier for them to do the right thing.

2. **Figure out where the organization is getting bad results from the path of least resistance.** Take a few minutes and think about specific situations where the organization is getting unwanted results because the easiest thing isn't the right thing. It's usually easy to spot waste, and a bit harder to see missed opportunities. Make a list of possibilities, and prioritize them by the impact they have or could have on the business. Brainstorm with people working in the affected area about how to add friction to help prevent mistakes.

3. **Use the force field, Luke.** Take a sheet of paper and create a force-field diagram,[32] titled with the challenge you want to tackle. Draw a vertical line in the center. On the left side, draw and label arrows representing all the mechanisms that support moving in the direction you want to go—physical, emotional, and mental. The bigger the force, the longer the arrow. On the right side, draw and label all the forces that are resisting forward progress.

Commuting by bike more often

Have a nice bike → | ← Takes longer

Want to exercise → |

| ← Needs tuneup

Wife likes to bike ⇒ | ← Bad weather

Then start taking action to remove or reduce the items on the right and increase or add items on the left. In my example of commuting by bike, buying a good rain jacket and tuning up the bike may be all I need to do to allow the forces on the left to gain the upper hand.

When you invest time up front to provide structure that makes the right action the default action, everyone wins every time that action takes place. Being deliberate about shaping your organization's design to use the path of least resistance everywhere possible can dramatically increase the energy and effort moving the organization forward.

How are you structuring the organization and people for success?

The extent to which you understand the design of the organization, as well as effective ways of fitting the moving parts together, determines your success and the success of the entire enterprise. This simple assessment can help you see how well you understand yourself in relation to the practices we just covered.

Look at each set of statements and mentally mark an X where you are on the continuum of that practice. Think of this more as a baseline than a report card. And don't cheat yourself—dishonest assessments will not be valuable to you.

Where are you right now on the following practices?

Practice 5.1 | **Use everyone's crayon in the picture**

| I decide the vision of where we need to go | I build ownership in a shared picture of the future | Whatever people envision is the direction we should go |

Practice 5.2 | **Know what's in the black box**

| I focus on what I can control - my job is to do my job | I work to understand how our organizational components interact | I know how the organization works better than anyone |

Practice 5.3 | **Work backward from the outcome**

| I dive in and start improving things from where we are | I work toward our shared picture of success | I won't allow changes unless we know the end result |

Practice 5.4 | **Make the right things easy**

Working hard to do the right thing is just what you have to do	I change the organization to make the right things easy	I encourage people to do whatever works for them

Consider these questions...

- Which practice stands out as important and urgent for you to address?

- How will working on it help you, others, and the organization?

- What's holding you back from working on it?

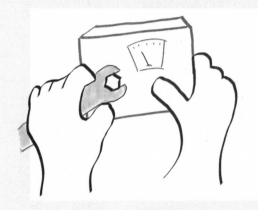

Principle 6

Organizations generating waste are generating opportunities for improvement

Principle 1
Leaders' effectiveness is proportional to how well they know themselves

Principle 2
Leaders are judged more by what they don't than by what they do

Principle 3:
People discover their best selves through being respected by a leader

Principle 4
People multiply a leader's power only as much as that power is shared

Principle 5
Organizations are designed to get the results they are getting

Principle 6

Organizations generating waste are generating opportunities for improvement

There are many different methods for designing and running your organization efficiently. Just a few examples: Lean Manufacturing, Six Sigma, Business Process Improvement, Theory of Constraints, Management by Objectives, and even Lean Six Sigma.[33] These methods use different tools and arrive at different outcomes, yet the idea behind them is roughly the same: optimize your organization's efficiency by removing waste, variation, and overload.

Improving efficiency is the last impact you can make before your stone skips out to the world beyond your organization. If you've aimed well and done the practices effectively up to this point, your stone—your effort—will have a lot of momentum and will also have created significant positive ripples with other people and the structure of the organization.

Reducing wasted effort and resources can make a immediate difference to overall performance. It's the fine tuning of the fuel, air, and spark system on the engine to get optimum efficiency and the best possible result given the resources available.

Squeezing everything out of a resource

My ten-year-old Honda Civic Hybrid car can easily carry four adults at highway speed for more than 600 miles on 13 gallons of fuel. If I play with some of the variables—turning off the air conditioning, braking as little as possible, accelerating very gently—I can stretch that range to more

Run and refine the organization to minimize waste and optimize output.

than 800 miles. While it's fun to get great mileage, I'm merely taking advantage of the design that allows this car to continuously adjust its fuel efficiency as we go. This system monitors and adjusts the efficiency of the engine many times each second, leading to amazing fuel efficiency that the system can sustain all the way to its first required tune-up at 100,000 miles.

While the design is self-adjusting, for the best result I have to make an effort to operate it efficiently. If I do jackrabbit starts and stops, I can cut my mileage in half in just minutes. To take advantage of the efficiency available in the system, I need to focus on running the system efficiently.

To optimize your organization's efficiency, there are four practices in this last principle of Ripple Leadership:

1. **Do or do not...there is no exception.** Run the organization systematically to improve it.

2. **Put a speedometer on everyone's dashboard.** Measure results and provide information that enables self-correction.

3. **Enable eggshell structure.** Focus on helping people do their best instead of preventing the worst.

4. **Go beyond status quo.** Either continuously learn and improve, or your organization will lose ground.

Each practice is focused on an important aspect of running your organization efficiently. They are part of a change loop that cycles through the organization, ultimately resulting in an organization that optimizes the results produced by you and others working within the structure.

If there is waste—that is, effort that doesn't result in value—it's an indication the organization is doing less than it is capable of. The best way to know where you need to adjust methods or redesign the structure is to do things exactly as designed and get data on the differences between desired and actual results.

Continuous improvement guru W. Edward Deming famously stated this formula for who's to blame when organizational problems arise: "94% belongs to the system (responsibility of management), 6% special [causes]."[34] As leaders, we need to avoid the common pitfall of looking for a person to blame, because the problem is mostly likely the system itself and therefore the person responsible is us.

Do or Do Not... there is NO Exception

Practice 6.1 | **Do or do not...there is no exception**

Take exception to exceptions—either change the system or just don't do it.

As you run your organization, it's important to continue to question the assumptions that were made when the system was built. To get optimum performance—that is, the maximum given the constraints and resources available—you must continually refine the system as you use it. This mindset is critical to get the most out of your organization, and to prevent the "way things are done" from hardening into what may become mindless and ineffective routines.

The goal, then, is to ensure integrity around the standards that keep organizations running smoothly and efficiently. Because when everything is an exception, nothing is an exception. Essentially, you no longer have a system when the system is nothing but exceptions.

Everything on rush, nothing's going anywhere

A visit to a high-tech manufacturing company highlighted the danger of allowing exceptions. My client was in charge of product development and was frustrated by the many moving parts of the organization that were holding his team back. We were discussing these challenges when suddenly he said, "You have to see this," grabbed me by the arm and walked me across campus to the manufacturing facility.

As we moved through the areas where metal was bent and formed for cases and housings, boards were assembled and soldered, and final product was being put together, I noticed red tags on many of the items. In some places nearly every item had a red tag. As we continued the

This practice is helpful if:

- **You are dealing with the same issues over and over again.**

- **Employees run on tribal knowledge, and work grinds to a halt when certain people are out.**

- **The organization is getting unpredictable results with high costs and long queue times.**

impromptu tour, my client described each step of the process to me with accompanying facts and figures about the products being made and where they were going—yet I was having a hard time focusing because all I could see were red tags. When we got to the end and were changing out of our protective gear, I asked about the tags. "You know, that's a funny thing," he said, a bit wistfully. "Those are rush tags to help us meet important customer deadlines. They worked at first, but now since most of our product is on rush, manufacturing has to spend extra time figuring out which rush components go together for which rush order. I think we may even be going slower than before!"

A few months later, the rush system was abandoned, and the plant worked to optimize the overall throughput instead of trying to make special exceptions for special customers.

The lesson here is that every time you say "Ok, I'll allow this just this once," you are almost always losing out. You're either hurting the integrity of your system or you're missing an opportunity to make a permanent improvement. Instead of giving in to the temptation of a one-time exception and starting down the path of death by a thousand cuts, surface the reasons an exception is being sought. If they are important enough, change the system to make this exception the rule.

Imagine your organizational structure as an earthen dam with a lot of pressure behind it. If you were to allow even a little water to go over where it's not intended, that water would quickly widen the pathway which would allow more water, which would widen the pathway more...until the dam is fully breached. If instead you either reinforced the dam a bit and didn't allow the water to leave, or better yet created a new concrete spillway that channels water over safely when a certain level is reached, your dam would stay intact and functioning for a long time.

Exercise 6.1 | **Reinforce the integrity of your system**

Running your organization so that the design is strengthened the more you use it is vital to having an organization everyone can rely on. These exercises will help you raise your awareness of where you may be slowly degrading the capacity of your organization because of the way you run the system.

1. **Examine your exception tolerance level.** How messy are you allowing your system to be? There can be a fine line between building on individual strengths and having exceptions be the rule. You may want to check with some of your trusted staff or colleagues if your tolerance level (or lack thereof) is negatively affecting the organization.

2. **Check your track record.** Divide a piece of paper into two columns to help you reflect on the performance of the organization. Title the left column "Results" and the right column "Reasons".

   a. List where you and your team are getting the results you expect and need.

   b. Add to the list where you and the team are not getting good results.

   c. Write your best guess for the reasons behind each success and failure in the right column.

   d. Finally, look for patterns that relate to how much the issue or the reasons were exceptions. Note them and start looking for opportunities to eliminate the exceptions in your system.

3. **Shift your system.** With the results of the previous exercise, take a few minutes and note the changes needed to increase system integrity going forward by incorporating any exceptions into the system. Pick a change that has the most significant impact for the least amount of effort, and work with your team to implement the change. Hint: the change needed is likely to be something your people have wanted to do for some time—you may have a hard time staying out of their way once you provide your team the authority to do something about it.

Part of achieving efficiency with your systems is to ensure you are looking at the outcomes first and adjusting as needed to get the result you really need. The next key is ensuring that everyone involved has information on the outcomes they are achieving so they can self-adjust to get better results.

PUT A SPEEDOMETER ON EVERYONE'S DASHBOARD

Practice 6.2 | **Put a speedometer on everyone's dashboard**

Feedback loops are one of the most powerful methods for self-driven performance improvement.

Many organizational leaders see their role as process police—pulling people over and giving them a ticket for violating the rules, providing a warning or punishment, then sending them on their way. The problem is that most of the time even when people are aware of the process, they have no idea what good (or bad) is supposed to look like, and furthermore have no way to measure their own performance. Employees are often blind-sided when their efforts get them into trouble.

I've heard about many annual performance reviews with employees who were operating in the dark without guidance or any way to get feedback until they had a conversation essentially like this:

Leader:	*"I'm glad we're having your review. You know you've been speeding the last several months, don't you?"*
Employee:	*"Really? Gosh, I didn't mean to. I thought I was doing ok. I didn't even know that I was speeding."*
Leader:	*"Yeah, well, I don't have time to put speed limit signs out, and besides, I wanted to let you run so I could see what you can really do. But there is a limit, and you were over."*
Employee:	*"Wow. Now that I know there's a limit, I'll be much more careful. But I am a bit confused— how I am supposed to know how fast I'm going without a speedometer?"*
Leader:	*"I've heard that one a lot too. But frankly I have quite a few other good people who seem to be able to just know when they're on track. And I'm a fair person—I let everyone know when they've exceeded the limit. Like you. And I truly hope you do better over the next six months Or else there will be greater consequences than this warning. Anything else I can do for you?"*

This practice is helpful if:

- You are reacting to isolated data points and believe you must navigate by gut feel.

- Employees take actions that appear disconnected from the results needed. When confronted they have no idea of the impact of their actions.

- The organization is wasting time and effort on activities and projects that go nowhere.

If it weren't so common it would be funny. Without feedback, there's no way to adjust to hit the goal. Even if someone manages to know what the goal is.

A metric in search of implementation

The closer a goal is to what an employee can influence, and the more information that employee has about how they are affecting needed outcomes, the more that employee is willing and able to adjust their inputs for better results.

I once worked at a high-tech firm that had experienced a decade of continuous growth of revenue and products. The executive leadership understood that the formation of silos and unhealthy competition between business units was a potential risk to continued growth. Their answer: unite everyone in the company with a shared goal tied to compensation in addition to their business unit performance goals. They selected Earnings Before Interest, Taxes, Depreciation, and Amortization, or EBITDA, and set a goal and a percentage of salary reward for everyone if we made the company goal. The goal was communicated at meetings, posted on the walls, and shared liberally with everyone. Our efforts were now united toward a common future.

Or so I thought until one evening I was working late and headed to the printer to find a fellow engineer dumping reams of paper into the trash. Apparently there was some problem with his file and rather than fix it he was pressing Reprint and then tossing the sheets that didn't print correctly. I shared that he was throwing our bonus in the trash, and he gave me a blank look. I explained further, "You know, the company EBIDTA goal. That paper you just tossed comes right off our bottom line and reduces our bonus!" He smirked at me, and replied "There's no way that paper will make a difference to how much money we make. It's just noise." He turned abruptly and walked off.

Admittedly the amount of money that paper represented was tiny compared to our topline revenue. Yet individuals not understanding how their actions affected bottom-line EBIDTA was exactly the problem the company was trying to combat! Until people cared enough about the impact of their actions and made changes, the company would continue suffering a death of a thousand cuts.

Incidentally, around that same time the company changed the system to reward more managers with stock options. This reward system was even more disconnected from what each person did every day. Sadly, as the tech bubble burst, people watched helplessly as their rewards became worthless even as they worked themselves harder and harder.

The incredible power of feedback loops

Feedback loops provide information about results in near-real time, providing people with the opportunity to adjust their actions to achieve the desired outcome.[36] You use feedback loops constantly and automatically—it's called your sensory and nervous system. Any delay or impairment of your personal feedback system can cause grave danger to you and anyone around you.

Organizational feedback loops have to be more deliberate and targeted to the specific result desired.

Take the proliferation of those "Your speed is" radar signs around schools. There's absolutely no new information on those signs—you know you're in a school zone (usually from the flashing lights), the speed limit is posted at 20 miles per hour, and you could look down and see what your actual speed is. But put all that information on a single sign that stays steadily lit, showing your speed if you're at or below the limit, flashes when you're over, and says SLOW DOWN when you're going over 25 miles per hour, and you get remarkable results. Most municipalities report 15-25% drop in average speed to under the speed limit. Perhaps there's a little peer pressure involved, yet there's no question that providing blatantly visible, real-time information makes a dramatic difference in this case.

To make sure that the goal you set and the measurement you are taking will result in real improvement, you must understand the entire system in which you are working. Or you might end up with a lot of effort without significant impact.

Just because the number changed, it doesn't mean you moved it

I once worked with a team focused on reducing costly scrap in a high-tech manufacturing plant. After several months of concerted effort, structured experiments and new methods, the team managed to achieve the goal of 20% scrap reduction. The results were projected to bring literally millions of dollars to the bottom line! So, I was surprised to find the lead engineer sitting alone in a corner *at the celebration party*, staring into his plastic cup of beer, looking pretty dejected.

When I asked him what was wrong, he mumbled something about having a funny feeling and running some reports that morning. He pushed some crumpled pieces of paper over to me. The reports showed that scrap had indeed been reduced by 20%, and sadly also showed that overall production had declined the same amount. This fellow didn't have the heart to interrupt the celebration to let the team know all their efforts essentially had made no real impact!

Likewise, as was illustrated earlier by the ***More is not always better*** graph, it's easy to get caught up in maximizing one metric or criteria at the expense of others. When working with executive teams that are caught up in conflict between organizational silos, I remind them of the following truth:

> *Optimizing an organization often requires suboptimizing the parts of that organization*

As discussed in ***Work backward from the outcome***, if any functional area is completely optimized—running in a perfectly efficient way—that optimization is more often than not at the expense of other functions and the organization as a whole. Even though many doctors and engineers and programmers hate "wasting time" documenting what they do or filling out paperwork, without that "inefficiency" the ultimate goals of healthy patients and safe systems and effective programs are very difficult to achieve. This isn't about zero-sum—it's about systemic dependencies of parts of the organization on each other.

To work well, your systems must provide everyone with the information *and understanding* to know what they need to do to be successful.

Exercise 6.2 | **Get everyone cruising**

These exercises are just the tip of the iceberg. It's one thing to improve people's awareness of standards and how they are performing to them. It's another to modify the system to provide people ongoing information and understanding to enable them to adjust as needed to hit the standard.

1. **Check your people's feedback equipment.** Enter into a dialogue with your key people around "What is success, and what do we need to know or have to achieve it?" Your goal is to increase your awareness as well as theirs of what we're aiming for, what information we get, and what that information is telling us or not telling us. Look for simple ways to create individual "Your Speed Is" information.

2. **Connect people to what's most important.** Pull out your company's vision, strategy, goals, and objectives. Make a quick list of the information you get that lets you know both you and the company are on track. Ask yourself how much of this everyone knows and understands. If you come up with some blanks, start a five-minute sharing session at each staff meeting to help people learn what matters.

3. **Start opening your window shades.** Determine what you could share that would help other people better understand the results and how they could make a difference personally. Choose one or two pieces of information and start sharing. Be sure to help people understand the "why behind the what" by asking questions that explore the impact beyond the numbers.

Once you've established effective feedback loops, you will be enabling people to correct their own behaviors to hit the goals. The next practice is about ensuring that the systems and resources, along with policies and procedures, are managed to enable the best in people instead of trying to simply reduce errors.

Practice 6.3 | **Enable eggshell structure**

Focus on helping people do their best instead of preventing the worst.

There are natural lifecycles of businesses that affect both what people focus on and the cost of that focus.

In startup mode, organizations are generally small and nimble, with everyone completely focused on doing just the right things to meet customer needs and generate revenue. Failures, when they occur, are seen as learning experiences to help the organization get the feedback it needs to pivot towards a more successful future.

As organizations grow, they develop a sense of pride around what they have accomplished and the hard-won methods of success they used to get there. This sense of pride becomes a double-edged sword—helping connect people to what creates more success, and at the same time causing people to begin fearing the loss of that success.

As a result, this pride of results and "the way we do things" can take on a life of its own. Failures, when they occur, begin to be seen as reasons to apply changes to "make sure we never make that mistake again." Well-intentioned structure begins to be applied to everything. Previously flexible controls and policies begin to take on the rigidity of steel beams and concrete columns. As the organizational fear of failure grows, people unconsciously accept that "the way we do things" is permanent and more-or-less inalterable, making changes and improvement difficult or impossible.

While it's important to have structure people can rely on, the problem is that too much structure throttles people's ability to be positively creative. People's innate creativity does find an outlet, yet gets channeled into getting their way *in spite* of the system instead of *through* the system.

This practice is helpful if:

- You are constantly frustrated with people who seem to fall short of what's needed.

- Employees complain and point out their colleagues' shortfalls.

- The organization makes edicts to handle problems that should be dealt with individually.

Energy is wasted on process instead of moving the organization forward, and the system has no way to get better.

Some leaders will claim that the structure must dictate every action to eliminate risk of failure. However, when structure eliminates the need to think and care about the outcomes we need, we get organizations that don't think and care about anything except the structure itself. And history has proven most self-focused organizations, even those that are very powerful and highly successful, eventually crumble under their own weight.

Why an eggshell?

To combat this tendency to overbuild structure, when we work with our clients, we aim instead for just what's needed and no more. We call this "eggshell structure," because eggshells are:

- Very thin compared to what they are enclosing.

- Semi-permeable, letting the right stuff in and keeping the bad stuff out.

- Strong enough to contain what is inside to help it fully develop and mature, yet easily broken from within to allow what's inside to grow to the next level.

To get eggshell structure you simply enclose what is currently happening and create a boundary for what shouldn't happen. It can be as simple as writing down what gets done each day on an office whiteboard to allow people to make sure everything gets done. Or figuring out our overarching goal together and deputizing everyone to ask "How is this meeting/project/method helping us get there faster/cheaper/better?" It's a stone that slips smoothly from your hand to glance the surface of the water and make just enough ripples to work for now and the next time.

Sadly, many organizations seem to put structure in place that instead shuts out the best efforts people have to offer. Without things like creativity, judgment, and artistry, an organization tends to become stodgy and bureaucratic—a place that sucks the life out of employees and customers alike.

A bank with too much structure

I was once a client of a national bank who-will-not-be-named that suffers this fate. Whenever I wanted to do something that was non-standard, the banker/agent would agree with me that it was a good idea, then would sadly share it was not possible because of this or that system or policy limitation. The situation was frustrating and corrosive. Eventually, the time came when I could not take it anymore. I am, after all, in the business of helping organizations enable excellence in their people and systems. Continuing to be a customer of this bank was simply too painful.

With my decision firm, I went to the bank and requested my accounts be closed. The banker asked me why and I told her honestly. She gave me a knowing look and said, "I understand, and frankly don't blame you." She turned back to her terminal, and after a moment of typing turned back with a resigned expression. "I'm extremely sorry. I'm afraid you can't close your business accounts here. You'll have to go to the central office because only they are allowed to do that." We both sat in silence for a moment, our heads bowed. The system had conquered us both.[36]

While this banker didn't hide behind the system, it is a powerful temptation for many leaders. A case in point was a commercial construction client I worked with on the East Coast.

How to disempower people and not get the results you want

One day I called to find the CEO fuming. "How can people be so inept? Don't they know the impact of what they're doing? Do people even care anymore?" He was so upset I was sure it was a significant project screw-up or worse, a workplace accident. His remarks were telling once I found out what it was really about.

"I've got two idiots who just cost us $500 in overage fees on our cell phone contract!" In response, he had already created a new policy with a hard limit for cell phone usage, and had angrily fired it off to everyone on his staff. There were just a few things he hadn't stopped to consider: the two people in question were project managers who did all their work via cell phone, all the other 22 project managers were actually under the limit he just established, and worst of all, no one but the CFO and CEO saw the actual statements on cellphone usage.

The result was that nearly everyone in the company was upset about being criticized—except for the two heavy users who didn't realize that the policy was aimed at correcting them! The CEO had attempted to use the structure to change behavior, yet did it in such a heavy-handed and impersonal way that people felt dehumanized.

Some leaders see systemic control as a black and white issue—either the system controls the people or we are out of control. They are unwilling to take the time to create structure that embraces the richness of human diversity and possibility. Yes, we need to have a system that helps shape the behavior of everyone involved. Yet for that system to be most effective, it should be designed to enable people to use it as a platform for their own individual and collective greatness.

A very simple example of this: an operator at a semiconductor plant noticed that the color was slightly different on the wafers as they went through her machines. While everything in the system showed the wafers were well within the standards and every prescribed test came out positive, she decided to give her process engineer a call to check things out before moving the product on. Turns out there was a mix up at the chemical plant, and that call prevented several million dollars of wasted material and effort. And that call happened because the leaders enabled this operator to go beyond the minimum.

People should not be at the mercy of the system—instead they should function as skilled mechanics, tweaking the system performance to optimal levels. Really good system mechanics treat policies and procedures as minimal guidelines, understanding how the system works, and how and when to go above and beyond. They know what the speedometer on their dashboard really means, and how to harness the system for everyone's benefit.

Exercise 6.3 | **Nurture skilled system mechanics**

The best people to help shape structure are those who are intimately involved with the results that structure produces. Understanding their experience is a very powerful way to make an organization simultaneously fit the people and what needs to get done.

1. **Find out how your organization is doing.** Put yourself in a prospect's, client's, or coworker's shoes. Ask yourself on a scale from 0-10 how well your organization is getting consistent results and at the same time encouraging the best from each person. Validate with a trusted team member or, better yet, a trusted customer or client. Be sure to keep your defenses down and openly explore the feedback you receive.

2. **Shift the way you engage with people around systemic issues.** Think about your top three organizational challenges. How could you engage people differently in solving them such that their best qualities would be called forth? Spend a few minutes each with three people finding out how they see the challenges. Your findings should be less about things to avoid and more about changes that will enable the right things to happen in the first place.

3. **Have a sacred cow barbecue.** Spend a few minutes thinking about which rule or process requirement simply no longer serves the organization or the people. Spend about twice as long validating your thoughts with a trusted agent. Change the rule—and be prepared to be mostly thanked and have at least one person complain that they liked it the old way.

If you've tackled even one exercise for each practice, you've started some big ripples in your organization, in your people, and in yourself. Yet the last practice ensures that we continue to pick up the right kind of pebbles to make the right kind of impacts that steadily move our organization and people forward. Maintaining everything at status quo is as possible as holding a ripple still.

Practice 6.4 | **Go beyond status quo**

Organizations naturally decline, so for optimum results, actively experiment and continuously tweak.

Status quo is the mythical state of things staying the same as they have been. This state is sought out by people who believe either: a) it's about as good as it's going to get, b) it may get worse so let's keep things the way they are, or c) people are just not willing to push the system because they want to stay in their comfort zone

Even if you've worked your way through every exercise in this book, and made dramatic improvements with the impact of your own personal, interpersonal, and organizational leadership, now is not the time to rest on your laurels.

Not that you wouldn't be in good company. The ancient Greeks started crowning heroes with laurels thousands of years ago, and people have rested on them ever since. The challenge is that once you've achieved a significant amount of success, you and everyone else in your organization are subject to the silent and unconscious conspiracy of focusing more on what you can lose than by what you might gain through change.

Perhaps you have experienced the difference between organizations focused on doing things right, and organizations focused on not doing things wrong. The former is making things happen and growing, while the latter is hunkering down and resisting change. It's natural that the more an organization has to lose, the greater the chance of desperately clinging to the ways things have been—which paradoxically takes the organization on a downward spiral toward oblivion.

This practice is helpful if:

- You see the same mistakes over and over again.

- Employees feel powerless and believe that their contributions have little to no effect. They may be cynical that any positive change is possible.

- The organization continues to experience preventable failures, and is losing customers and good employees as a result.

> What gets measured gets done, what gets measured and fed back gets done well, what gets rewarded gets repeated
>
> John E. Jones

I believe there is really no such thing as status quo, and that you're either growing or declining in some way. If you agree, I strongly recommend you consciously choose the path of continuous improvement upward. Otherwise you're unconsciously choosing the path of slow decline.

The Ripple Effect itself also demonstrates how there cannot be a status quo. Ripples don't happen by themselves—stones have to fly smoothly through the air and skip off water to create them. Once set in motion, these ripples spread and slowly diminish. Without engagement the water naturally becomes still and passive. Your organization needs your intentional and ongoing improvement or it too will diminish.

Improve the system by changing what you're focusing on

Just as a leader needs to **Risk and be resilient**, the organization itself needs to take chances to get better. Remember the lesson from the old cabinetmaker: "You can make it perfect, or you can make it adjustable." For organizations, perfection is best approached through continuous adjustment and improvement.

Continuous improvement is a buzz-phrase that actually means something. The continuous part doesn't mean every single second—it means a steady, sustained effort over time. Changes take a while to implement, and getting real results requires making many small experiments and tweaks.

It's critical to focus at the right frequency for the level of challenge in the organization. From my perspective, the more important an outcome is for the long-term success of your organization, the less you should need to measure and tweak it. The most important things—like why your organization exists—are almost timeless; while frequent reminders are handy, adjustments should be extremely rare. As we move further away from what's most important to achieve long-term success and how the organization should do it, measurements and adjustments should increase in frequency.

Here's an example of a company looking at financial results—the top are important outcomes and the bottom is a time spectrum.

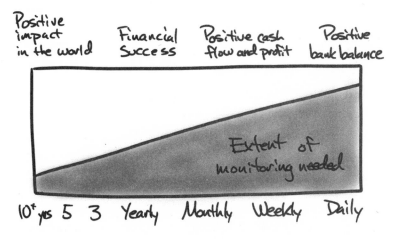

So this says we need to monitor bank balances frequently, while keeping in mind the big picture of having a net positive impact on the world. The more general model then looks like:

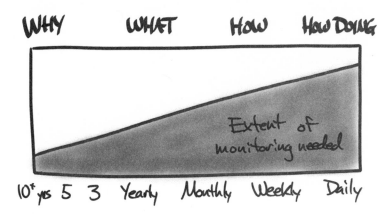

It's not enough to simply monitor and measure. To get real improvement we have to make sure the right feedback loops are present and working in the system.

How to continuously improve—the right way

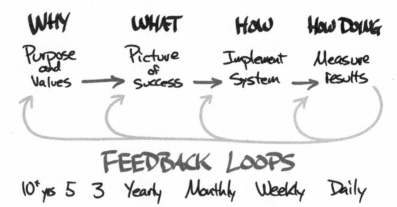

Just like it's important to ***Put a speedometer on everyone's dashboard*** so that everyone can understand their impact and self-adjust, we need the right feedback loops for the organization to identify where it needs to adjust. The difference is that we are focused on improving the results rather than resting on our laurels and simply meeting the standard. We want to see if we can set a new one.

By setting a new standard we can leverage the reality that people are more motivated by potential loss than potential gain.[37] The potential loss of not meeting a new standard (as long as it's legitimate and not contrived) will generally encourage people to get more creative than if you simply ask them to do better.

For example, our team was doing some teambuilding work once where we had a complicated task involving a rope circle, 30 Frisbees, and touching them in order. After the first run, we tweaked the process, got about 20% improvement, then tweaked the process again for another 5%. We had one run left.

"What if I told you the record was less than half of your fastest time?" the instructor gently taunted. First we were incredulous, then after we realized she was serious, we got serious too. Our team worked quickly to completely redesign our approach, and our last run, while not record breaking, took half as long as our best previous performance.

American executives and workers who visited Japanese production plants in the 1980s had the same shock, and were virtually forced to rethink their approach to be able to compete with a new world standard. The Toyota Production methodology, now known more broadly as Lean Manufacturing, is being applied throughout organizations to enable workers at all levels of the organization to improve processes through feedback and experimentation. Setting a reachable, ever-increasing standard is a powerful tool for overall improvement. But where do you start improving?

Prioritize outcomes—biggest impact and most doable first

Determining what's important and what's not is one of the biggest challenges for leaders. Fortunately there are more than a few tools to help you hone your focus to make the most of the time, energy, and resources you have to improve results.

An Italian economist named Vilfredo Pareto noticed 20% of the pea pods in his garden contained 80% of the peas, then he noticed 80% of the land was owned by 20% of the people—and the Pareto Principle was born.[38] This simple rule of thumb can help you start working on the critical few problems that have the biggest impact on results. If you graph the impact of issues in an organization, by people or revenue or whatever else is important, it will look something like this:

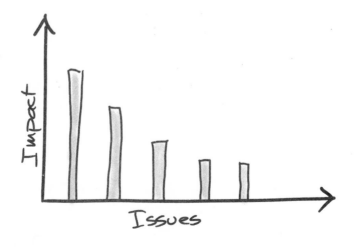

The way to start working these issues is the biggest impact first. By focusing your effort and that of the organization on the critical few problems that have the majority of the impact on desired results, you will keep everyone focused on what's most important.

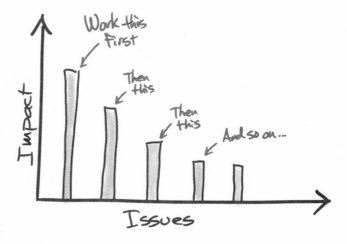

Since data can mislead, be sure to get input from people who experience the issues and benefits firsthand. Because they are the ones doing the work, they are the most likely to know the real symptoms. Then you can design and run experiments with them to figure out how to do things better. In my experience, most of the best ideas come from those who are dealing with the real processes and work.

A recent client of ours, in business for more than 50 years, decided it was time to create their first 5-year strategic plan. Once the leadership team got the important clarifying questions answered about Why they exist, What they value, What they do, and What's important,[39] that context gave new life to an idea that had been floating around in the business for a while—doing an operational review. A cross-functional team got together and asked front line people what's working, what's not, and what could be done better. The information gathered resulted in changes that reduced costs 20-30% in some areas of the business. By tackling the most common challenges, this team got immediate benefit even as part of a long-range plan.

While improvement efforts can save money and help people, it's also important to know when to stop improving.

Avoid overcontrol and churn

In my experience, it's very easy for leaders and technical experts to get caught up in a fruitless search for certainty and perfection.[40] After all, if a little improvement is good, then a lot must be really great, right? (Remember *More is not always better?*) There are probably a lot of reasons for this—a desire to add value, a need to feel competent, avoiding hard choices, not wanting to fail. Regardless of the reason, to prevent wasted effort, frustration, and needless delays you'll need to keep the effort as small, quick, and nimble as possible.

Here are a few ways to do this:

- **Wrestle with the desired outcomes and benefits before you start problem solving.** Then sketch out what you know the problem is and isn't, along with what you know and don't know. Experiment to find the unknown information needed to be able to achieve the outcomes.

- **When you're working on a problem or are trying to make an improvement, validate the need for it with real data.** Objective information—hard data—is best. Second best is using an objective process to collect people's subjective opinions.

- **Start as small as possible.** A great approach is to aim for Minimum Viable Offer[41]—that is, doing the absolute minimum amount of effort needed to prove or disprove your idea. Once you have proof-of-concept, then ramp up investing to achieve the results you need.

> In anything at all, perfection is finally attained, not when there is no longer anything to add, but when there is no longer anything to take away.
>
> Antoine de Saint-Exupery

- **Benchmark other organizations that (you think) are doing it
  better than you.** Start with your industry, then look for dissimilar
  organizations trying to get similar outcomes.

- **Leverage continuous quality improvement tools such as Value
  Stream Mapping, Lean, or Six Sigma**. Consider systemic tools like
  Baldrige or ISO.

Once you start down the path of continuous improvement, there's no
turning back. As people begin to think more about the results and their
approaches, you will create momentum that enables everyone to improve
the systems and processes.

Exercise 6.4 | **Use your laurels as a springboard for the future**

The excellence you've helped make happen in your organization will set a new standard—not just in the results you've gotten, but also in the confidence of the team in creating their own future. Your continued role is therefore to keep providing gentle, consistent pressure toward increased levels of excellence. As Oliver Cromwell once said, "He who stops being better stops being good."

1. **Celebrate a recent success.** Publicly recognize a person or team who has made an improvement that impacted results. This will also have the Ripple Effect of encouraging others to make improvements. [Note: If you have a difficult time finding something to celebrate, either you are already doing everything perfectly, or your organization may be too difficult to change. In the latter case, try knocking down barriers—see *Make the right things easy.*

2. **Evaluate how you track success.** Review how important goals, objectives, and metrics are tracked and provided to the organization, and the frequency of measurements. How do we know when things are going well or are going poorly? How certain are we of a real trend, and that we're tracking the right information? Are the measurements timely enough to make adjustments and improve results? If needed, take action to improve the quality system of measurements, feedback, and adjustment. Resist the urge for perfect solutions—just make things better.

3. **Figure out where your benchmarks are.** Write a list of organizations in your industry that you would like to emulate. Add other organizations that operate under similar conditions—for example, Southwest Airlines benchmarked NASCAR pit crews to figure out how to fuel and turn their planes faster![42] Think about the results you'd like to achieve and you can find great examples in unusual places. Another benefit if you cross industries is that you're more likely to get cooperation and breakthrough ideas.

4. **Conduct Lessons Learned reviews.** Developed by the US Army, simple reviews at the end of each exercise or project can help organizations remind themselves what went well, what went poorly, how would we do it differently next time, and who needs to know. Taking a few minutes at the end of a meeting to find out what the group would like to Start doing, Stop doing, and Continue doing can make an amazing difference to the next and subsequent meetings.

By ensuring the organization pays attention to results and has the confidence to make changes to itself, you will be creating what Peter Senge defines as a learning organization[43]—that is, an organization that can flex and change as needed to make the impact it exists to make on the world.

Self-Assessment

How are you influencing the organization to get better and better?

The extent you can influence how well organizational systems are run will determine how consistent and efficient everyone can be working together. This next simple assessment can help you see how well you are influencing the organization in relation to the practices we just covered.

Look at each set of statements and mentally mark an X where you are on the continuum of that practice. Think of this more as a baseline than a report card. And don't cheat yourself—dishonest assessments will not be valuable to you.

Where are you right now on the following practices?

Practice 6.1 | **Do or do not...there is no exception**

| I allow exceptions if there are special circumstances | I allow exceptions as long as they are made permanent | I enforce the process and rules no matter what |

Practice 6.2 | **Put a speedometer on everyone's dashboard**

| My job is to tell people when they are off target | I make sure people have the information to self-regulate | The numbers dictate what we need to do |

Practice 6.3 | **Enable eggshell structure**

| The structure makes decisions for everyone, including me | I make sure our structure encourages the best in people | I make sure our structure doesn't get in the way of anyone |

Practice 6.4 | **Go beyond the status quo**

| If it isn't broken, I don't fix it | I'm constantly tweaking what and how we do things | I break things so we have to fix them |

Consider these questions...

- Which practice stands out as important and urgent for you to address?

- How will working on it help you, others, and the organization?

- What's holding you back from working on it?

Important points about leading the organization

Reflection and repetition allow us to learn lessons from what we've already heard, read, and done. Here's a summary of the important points from the section on Leading the Organization:

Principle 5
Organizations are designed to get the results they are getting

Use everyone's crayon in the picture
When people see their influence in a shared vision of the future, they become owners.

Know what's in the black box
An understanding of your organization's parts and connections is required to help everything work together.

Work backward from the outcome
Start with where you want to end up, then trace back each preceding step to today.

Make the right things easy
Create systems that get the best result by default, and make the worst result hard to achieve.

Principle 6
Organizations creating waste are generating opportunities for improvement

Do or do not...there is no exception
Take exception to exceptions—either change the system or just don't do it.

Put a speedometer on everyone's dashboard
Feedback loops are one of the most powerful methods for self-driven performance improvement.

Enable eggshell structure
Focus on helping people do their best instead of preventing the worst.

Go beyond status quo
Organizations naturally decline—so for optimum results, actively experiment and continuously tweak.

How to start moving forward

Congratulations! You've completed the first step of your journey. Now the real work begins.

If you've ever learned to drive a manual transmission or speak a foreign language, you know that new skills take time. At first, even trying things out feels very mechanical and awkward. You make mistakes. You think about the right thing to do or say long after it's appropriate to do so. You feel dumb, stupid, and incompetent. If you're like most adults who place a significant amount of value in their own competence, this kind of effort feels like self-inflicted torture. It's physically, mentally, and emotionally painful.

And that barrier to entry is the reason you'll be far ahead of the rest of the crowd if you decide to persist.

Throughout this book, I use phrases like "Most leaders..." and "Many people..." because in my experience, committed excellence to leadership is rare. Ripple Leaders are rare. Most people (there I go again) give up when the going gets tough.

Yet now that you know what's possible, I hope you're more willing than most to give it a try. The key is to get your first small win as soon as possible.

Rewiring both my house and my brain

My wife and I bought a house in our hometown of Fort Collins sight unseen. We were in Massachusetts, planning our return back to Colorado in a few years, and wanted to secure a house we could remodel into the home we wanted.

Three years later we moved back and started working on changing our 1937 single-story ranch into a two-story farmhouse, complete with porches, a harvest kitchen, and room for our whole family. About a year later, I was standing in one of the older bedrooms, connecting the wiring in the new portion of the house with the original existing wiring, when the insulation on those wires crumbled where I touched it. I was stunned.

Since this wiring was in metal conduits, we would have to rewire the entire existing house, and probably remove much of the conduit, and replace many of the wall boxes because of how they were set up, and...the list rolled out of my head onto the floor. Both my wife and I were working during the day and doing remodeling at night, we were trying hard to get the house finished, and we did not have extra funds to hire an electrician.

I felt the weight of the additional work pile onto my shoulders until I literally slid down the wall and found myself sitting on the floor. I sat there quietly for a few moments, feeling despair creeping in. How was I going to do this task that felt, in that moment, next to impossible?

I looked up and saw a light switch on the wall next to me. I'd already pulled new wires for the fan and light combination, and the thought occurred to me: "I can't wire the house, but I can wire this switch." And I did. Once it was done, I thought I'd check it, so I went out to close the breaker, came back in, and flipped the switch. Light filled the room, and I felt a ray of hope. The next thought that occurred was: "If I can wire this switch and make it work, I can wire another one." And I did. Eventually I rewired the whole house, bit by bit. I don't know how I got lucky enough to pick a light switch first, yet the immediate feedback I got made a huge difference to my faith in myself.

Based on my experience with the light switch and working with other clients, I highly recommend choosing something for your first project that you can readily accomplish *and* that will provide you with hopeful, positive feedback to build momentum for a series of wins.

Once you start "winning," your confidence will rise and you will have more forward momentum to make it through the minor setbacks and challenges that will come your way.

If you get stuck, back down the mountain a bit until you find a spot with more traction, then give it another run. Use your notes and revisit sections that continue to challenge you. Try the self-assessments or use the ***BUT I NEED HELP NOW!*** to zero in on which practice might be most helpful in your situation.

Whatever you do, don't give up. Reach out to peers or trusted advisors to get support through the rough spots. Everyone has them. As I've heard before, it's not how many times you fall down, but how many times you get up.

I wish you the best.

P.S. Visit rippleleader.com for a free workbook, templates, summary, and other useful tools

BUT I NEED HELP NOW!

Over time, I've learned to value the power of diagnostics. People I turn to for help—whether my doctor, my mechanic, or my leadership coach—ask me questions that quickly get to the heart of whatever I'm dealing with. This process enables me to minimize pain and struggle, and save time and money.

In the diagnosis process, I get asked questions about my observations of the situation at hand. More often than not, the choices presented increase my understanding of my own situation more clearly at the same time they guide my helpers to a diagnosis.

This guide is built to help you diagnose which practice would help you most in your situation.

The organization in this section mirrors that of the book—by principle and more specifically by practice—with typical symptoms seen by the leader (you), in yourself, others, and the organization.

Some symptoms appear multiple times since these practices are built to help improve multiple symptoms. (Imagine how many different conditions a doctor would uncover by asking "Does it hurt?") Make sure you don't stop at the first symptoms that resonate with you. Instead, skim through the rest of the list to see which feels most like what you're dealing with.

How to use this quick diagnostic guide

This guide is meant to help you self-diagnose challenges and start working on relatively simple enhancements to your leadership to get better results. It's something like walking a beach or lakeshore with lots of smooth, round pebbles—which pebbles you pick up depend on what you want to achieve. To get your Ripple going, you need to decide what you're going to aim at first, and which practices you want to become more proficient in.

You'll notice that some of the symptoms overlap—often that's because similar challenges show up at the personal, interpersonal, and organizational leadership levels.

As you build your skills in all three areas, revisit this list often. Leadership development is something of a spiral—you'll likely see similar issues again and again, yet as you gain skills you'll reencounter them at different levels and build new capabilities as you get better at handling the issues you're facing right now.

1. **Skim through the list and find symptoms that closely match what you are experiencing. Be aware that there may be more than one set that applies.**

2. **Go to the section with the applicable practice. Read through the section and try at least one exercise to see if you get better results.**

3. **Lather. Rinse. Repeat as needed.**

Principle 1
Leaders' effectiveness is proportional to how well they know themselves

PRESENTING SYMPTOMS	You find people guessing what you want—and they're often wrong.
	Employees are forming "us versus them" camps and taking things more personally than is helpful.
	The organization is underperforming to your expectations.
PRACTICE	*Decide what matters most* (page 25)

PRESENTING SYMPTOMS	You are constantly opportunistic and nothing lasts long before the next better opportunity comes along.
	Employees complain they are constantly subjected to the "flavor of the month," and you don't see people committing to change.
	The organization is splintered with functions working toward different goals.
PRACTICE	*Chart your own course* (page 31)

PRESENTING SYMPTOMS	You are surprised / disappointed other people can't do the things you can.
	Employees question their own abilities, and prejudge others' abilities.
	The organization is slow to respond to where you think it should be.
PRACTICE	*Know where you're awesome* (page 39)

Principle 2
Leaders are judged more by what they don't than by what they do

PRESENTING SYMPTOMS	You are a happy firefighter fueled by and addicted to urgency.
	Employees are complaining of "whiplash" from constant changes of direction.
	Lots of activity is occurring in the organization, yet not much progress is being made.
PRACTICE	*Do the hard stuff* (page 54)

PRESENTING SYMPTOMS	You find yourself living out "Groundhog Day"—experiencing the same challenges again and again with no relief or improvement.
	Employees do lots of could've/would've/should've second-guessing.
	The organization is often "overcome by circumstances" where a decision is no longer needed since the situation dictates what must be done.
PRACTICE	*Risk and be resilient* (page 59)

PRESENTING SYMPTOMS	You find yourself burning the candle at both ends and the middle— with occasional illness forcing you to take time off.
	Employees are getting burnt out and are stepping down or leaving.
	The organization is going faster than anyone can keep up with.
PRACTICE	*Charge your own batteries* (page 66)

Principle 3
People discover their best selves through being respected by a leader

PRESENTING SYMPTOMS	You find others delaying doing what you ask, subtly undermining, or even overtly engaging against your efforts.
	Employees are behaving badly—from not speaking directly about problems, to working around certain people, to even walking out of meetings or threatening others (usually done defending their function to hide personal animosity).
	The organization moves forward at a snail's pace with great expense of energy, work, and money. Schedules are slipped, budgets run over, sales are missed, and good people leave for greener pastures.
PRACTICE	*Trust or have nothing* (page 88)

PRESENTING SYMPTOMS	You find people responding to your requests with "What's in it for me / my team?"
	Employees are either vocal about getting their needs met, or say what they need to say to then do whatever they want.
	The organization rebuffs internal and external customers—pays them lip service and takes care of itself first. Customers stay only as long as they feel they don't have an option, and bad-mouth the company when asked about you.
PRACTICE	*Mission first. Others second. You? Last* (page 93)

PRESENTING SYMPTOMS	You find yourself mentally writing people off—or worse complaining to people about someone else's limitations
	Employees seem to put people "in a box"—limiting their potential to what's they have seen or assumed they have seen.
	The organization is complacent—settling for "what is" in terms of performance.
PRACTICE	*Assume most of your stories are wrong* (page 100)

PRESENTING SYMPTOMS	You are constantly focused on fixing flaws, stomping out failure wherever it starts to show up.
	Employees talk about people's personal and organizational shortfalls— gossip runs rampant to find the next negative focus.
	The organization settles for complacency, with language like "Good enough for government work" and "That's just the way it is."
PRACTICE	*Look for the diamonds in the dirt* (page 107)

PRESENTING SYMPTOMS	You are disappointed that you are the only one who seems to care enough to really understand what the business is about.
	Employees aren't thinking for themselves, and are unaware of the implications of their actions and decisions.
	The organization seems to learn lessons the hard way, and often require heroic efforts to resolve problems.
PRACTICE	*Help them figure out how to fish* (page 111)

Principle 4
People multiply a leader's power only as much as that power is shared

PRESENTING SYMPTOMS	You are irritated that you have to slow down; that others can't keep up with you; that you somehow ended up with the wrong people.
	Employees can't keep up to your standards, and are constantly making errors and missing opportunities.
	The organization is constantly slipping deadlines, and you often find out about problems after they are too far gone to recover from gracefully.
PRACTICE	*Meet them at eye level* (page 127)

PRESENTING SYMPTOMS	You find yourself trying to figure out or guess where the team really is, then scramble to adjust.
	Employees hesitate, appearing not to know what to do next, or they are just doing whatever they want with little connection to what's really needed.
	The organization doesn't go anywhere while you're away or not involved—you have to be there to push. Or you feel you have no influence and (bad) things are happening that you can't seem to get in front of.
PRACTICE	*Lead from a half step ahead* (page 133)

PRESENTING SYMPTOMS	You spend time with people then find your strength drained and they're recharged. It's almost like you are other people's battery.
	Employees seem to be dragging at work, going through the motions without any real interest, and very little commitment to anything beyond the bare minimum.
	The organization seems to be on a very slow treadmill.
PRACTICE	*Light their torches* (page 141)

PRESENTING SYMPTOMS	You wonder why people aren't getting things done—people constantly come back to you for everything.
	Others complain they can't do their jobs or they settle for the way things are with a fatalistic attitude. "We've got what we've got, so live with it."
	Organizational focus is on keeping people equal versus tapping individual strengths for the good of the whole.
PRACTICE	*Be their outfitter and guide* (page 149)

Principle 5
Organizations are designed to get the results they are getting

PRESENTING SYMPTOMS	You have a clear picture of where the organization and people could go, yet no one seems inspired or interested. It's like pushing sand up a rope.
	Employees compete to come out on top with other sections or people, especially by withholding information and helpful effort.
	The organization has pockets of excellence, yet at times is working at cross purposes.
PRACTICE	*Use everyone's crayon in the picture* (page 169)

PRESENTING SYMPTOMS	You are constantly working problems yet feel like you're just putting on Band-Aids.
	Employees put the results of their section or function ahead of the organization.
	The organization tends to approach every problem as completely unique.
PRACTICE	*Know what's in the black box* (page 177)

PRESENTING SYMPTOMS	You are not sure what levers to pull to get the results you need.
	Employees focus solely on getting their function to look good and meet their goals, despite other functions' needs.
	The organization is busy yet not producing the results needed.
PRACTICE	*Work backward from the outcome* (page 185)

PRESENTING SYMPTOMS	You find yourself cutting corners because the right things take too long.
	Employees take the low road—even worse, people are kept when they violate standards yet get results.
	The organization is making mistakes that in hindsight were very preventable, and procedure exceptions are the norm.
PRACTICE	*Make the right things easy* (page 191)

Principle 6
Organizations generating waste are generating opportunities for improvement

PRESENTING SYMPTOMS	You are dealing with the same issues over and over again.
	Employees run on tribal knowledge, and work grinds to a halt when certain people are out.
	The organization is getting unpredictable results with high costs and long queue times.
PRACTICE	*Do or do not...there is no exception* (page 205)

PRESENTING SYMPTOMS	You are reacting to isolated data points and believe you must navigate by gut feel.
	Employees take actions that appear disconnected from the results needed. When confronted they have no idea of the impact of their actions.
	The organization is wasting time and effort on activities and projects that go nowhere.
PRACTICE	*Put a speedometer on everyone's dashboard* (page 209)

PRESENTING SYMPTOMS	You are constantly frustrated with people who seem to fall short of what's needed.
	Employees complain and point out their colleagues' shortfalls.
	The organization makes edicts to handle problems that should be dealt with individually.
PRACTICE	*Enable eggshell structure* (page 215)

PRESENTING SYMPTOMS	You see the same mistakes over and over again.
	Employees feel powerless and believe that their contributions have little to no effect. They may be cynical that any positive change is possible.
	The organization continues to experience preventable failures, and is losing customers and good employees as a result.
PRACTICES	*Go beyond status quo* (page 221)

Thanks and appreciation

This book could not be in your hands without the help of many other people.

First and greatest appreciation goes to my life partner, Diana Hutchinson, for her tireless support and encouragement. Many of the lessons I've learned were provided to me by my children, Sara, Rebecca, Brian, and Sophia— powerful teachers and apt pupils.

Thanks to everyone who's been part of our success at Trebuchet Group— Josh Schuler, Bekki Smith, Steve Marshall, Grace Cooley, Ruth Pankratz, Carole Crane, Lee Porter, Mary Gallagher-Stanislo, Carol Chavez, Hill Grimmett, Ann Alexander, Kevin Houchin, Lisa Poshusta-Gregory, Lindsay Ogden, Andy Wibbels, Kim Kortum, Nina East, Ray Taylor, and other past members of the team.

Professional support comes from my mentor, friend, and coach Richard Reardon, my editors Matthew Gartland of WinningEdits.com and Karla Oceanak of Bailiwick Press, my publishing coach Josh Kaufman of personalmba.com, my cover designer and layout guru Launie Parry, and the person who introduced me to coaching, Sara Hurd.

Thanks to the editing and review team members Leta Behrens, Gretel Enck, Ben Kimbell, Carol Krismann, Joel Larner, Steve Mahlers, Chris Otto, Anne Walker, and Tim Whetter.

There are a host of giants—thought leaders whose shoulders I stand on, including:

- Seth Godin—for inspiration to be a courageous and generous artist and to just ship it

- Patrick Lencioni—for practical perspective and validation of being a naked consultant

- Peter Block—for simple and powerful applied philosophy of serving others

- James Kouzes and Barry Posner—for doing all that research on leaders so I didn't have to

- Thomas Leonard—who connected me with coaching, Richard Reardon, and my personal passion

- Stephen R. Covey—for helping me get my priorities straight

I could not have done this without all our clients at Trebuchet Group, who enable us to do our best work, teach us where we need to improve, and support us in helping others. Every one of our clients is amazing, and I want to call out special appreciation for: Paul Beiser, Josh Birks, Jenny Briggs, Kathy Collier, Doug Dwyer, Bob Flynn, Ed Harvey, Bruce Hendee, Ben Kimbell, Ken Kumph, Bob LaFort, Joel Larner, Chris Otto, Christine Perich, Kelly Peters, Terry Phelan, Doug McCarthy, Jay Richardson, Lisa Rosintoski, Ray Schofield, Jim Spencer, Jenn Vervier, Anne Walker, and Tim Whetten.

And finally, a special thank you to all my colleagues, mentors, and teachers at school, work, and community organizations who taught me so much, and more often than not gave me the opportunity to fail and learn from my mistakes. Because they all cared enough to develop me, I am able to share and continue refining my own learning for my clients, colleagues, and family.

Endnotes

These references just scratch the surface of the powerful information contained in the articles and books listed. I wholeheartedly recommend any material from the authors and people referenced.

1. **Laws of leadership**. Starting in 1982, James Kouzes and Barry Posner set out to create a simple, effective, and validated framework for leadership, and have since written four editions of *The Leadership Challenge*. The first time I saw the five leadership practices in the book, I was amazed at how effectively all my experience with leaders both good and bad fit their model. James' and Barry's research and thinking have strongly shaped my thinking about helping leaders understand what leadership is about. We frequently use their online 360-degree Leadership Practices Inventory in our executive coaching. Bonus: if you want to get the same principles and practices in a shorter format, I recommend their 2010 book *The Truth about Leadership: The No-fads, Heart-of-the-Matter Facts You Need to Know*.

2. **Without vision, the people perish**. *The Bible*, Proverbs 29:18. Ancient wisdom describing the vital need for people to have hope for a purpose and future. Even when faced with terrible circumstances, if people see a purpose for being they are more likely to be able to work toward achieving that purpose. Without purpose, people can lose the will to continue.

3. **Start with the end in mind.** In my opinion, the most readable of Stephen Covey's books is *First Things First* (1996). Writing with A. Roger Merrill and Rebecca Merrill, Stephen elaborates on the second habit of

highly effective people to help others understand how to effectively separate the important from the unimportant. I am definitely a Coveyite, reading all his books and using systems inspired by the habits to manage my priorities to get to the end results I desire. I was fortunate to meet Dr. Covey in person once, and can tell you he was as personable as can be.

4. **Discerning life purpose.** In *Inspire! What Great Leaders Do* (2004), Lance Secretan writes about finding your Destiny (Why I am here on Earth), Cause (How I will be while I am here and what I will stand for) and Calling (What I will do and how I will use my talents and gifts to serve). I got to meet Lance in person after a speech he gave, and shared that his talk inspired me more than I had been in some time. As he gave me a warm handshake, he smiled and said "Well, you need to be inspired more often!"

5. **Be the change you wish to see in the world.** Though this quote is disputed and may be a paraphrase of other words from Mahatma Gandhi, to me it is clearly aligned with the way Gandhi lived out his life. A story I've read is that this quote comes from a time when Gandhi was approached by a mother and child, asking him to exhort her son to give up sweets. Gandhi asked her to come back in a few weeks, which she did. "Give up sweets," Gandhi instructed the son. The mother, confused, asked Gandhi why he didn't just say that the last time they were there. "Madam, I had to first give up sweets."

6. **Building on strengths versus fixing weaknesses.** Marcus Buckingham has written several books on strengths, leveraging survey data to help people look for what they do best. I believe being aware of natural strengths (habits, tendencies, abilities) is important in figuring out what we're best at, and noticing what's not working can enable us to use our strengths for best results.

7. **As a leader, more isn't always better.** In *What Got You Here Won't Get You There: How Successful People Became Even More Successful* (2007), Marshall Goldsmith outlines twenty habits where leaders carry their

successful past practices into situations where those practices no longer add value, and how to achieve positive change. This book has helped leaders I work with self-identify what everyone around them could benefit from if they did less.

8. **Assessments—which are best?** To me, the best assessments provide insight into yourself that enables you to tap strengths and minimize weaknesses—in other words, be more aware of who you are and how you can more effectively work with others. It is challenging to find assessments that can provide language around strengths without inadvertently labeling people. Our primary assessments tools are: Target Training International's Talent Insights to understand personality styles and motivators, Thomas-Kilmann Conflict Inventory to understand conflict styles, and the Leadership Practices Inventory 360 to understand leadership behaviors. For teams, we also use Table Group's Team Assessment to understand team functionality.

9. **The history of you, a decade at a time.** *The Journal 10+* by Ian Matthews gives you the ability to see eleven years worth of information for each calendar date. What I like best is the fact that each entry has just 3 lines, so there's minimal effort required. Included are yearly goal pages, monthly summary pages, and even overflow pages so you can write longer notes when a particular day involves a breakthrough or extra challenge. I'm on my second journal, and the self-understanding it provides when I use it is invaluable.

10. **Will Rogers.** My favorite philosopher/humorist. If you ever have a chance, go to the Will Rogers Memorial in Claremont, Oklahoma, and be prepared to stay a while. Until then, look him up in Wikipedia. Another great quote: "There are three kinds of men. The ones that learn by readin'. The few who learn by observation. The rest of them have to pee on the electric fence for themselves."

11. **Stuck in the thick of thin things.** Stephen Covey, in his classic book *The Seven Habits of Highly Effective People* first published in 1989 introduces time-tested principles which can dramatically improve

individual effectiveness. I think we all get caught up in the "tyranny of the urgent" and benefit from shifting our focus to what's important versus what's simply calling for our attention.

12. **The enemy of the best is often the good.** Another Covey quote, encouraging us not to settle for where we are. At the other end of the spectrum is Voltaire's quote "Perfect is the enemy of good" –providing wisdom that the search for perfection is often fruitless. The ideal state is somewhere between just good and perfect.

13. **Activation energy.** Researcher Shawn Achor pulls together research in the field of positive psychology in a way that makes it very accessible to everyone. Don't believe me? Just watch his TED talk on how he started his career convincing his sister that she was a baby unicorn. http://www.ted.com/talks/shawn_achor_the_happy_secret_to_better_work

14. **Don't prepare, just show up.** My copy of Patricia Ryan Madson's book *Improv Wisdom* (2005) looks like a mouse attacked it because there are so many dog-eared pages. Patricia's counter-intuitive approach to build confidence in yourself and others involves getting more comfortable with not knowing what's going to happen next and being open to the gifts that will emerge from the chaos that is life.

15. **Gratitude.** There are quite a few studies out there on the topic. I liked a more personal article from *Inc. Magazine* contributor Dave Kerpen on practical application of gratitude in today's fast-paced business world: "The Legal Drug That Nobody's Talking About." http://www.inc.com/dave-kerpen/the-legal-drug-that-nobodys-talking-about.html

16. **Wikipedia.** If you don't know about it, you may have been living under a rock for the last few years. There's even a page where you can see edits in real-time, with the article and geographic location of the editor highlighted on a world map. Fascinating! http://rcmap.hatnote.com/#en

17. **Path to Action model.** If you don't know the VitalSmarts guys—Kerry Patterson, Joseph Grenny, Ron McMillan, Al Switzer—you should.

They've written a suite of practical and helpful books to increase people's ability to communicate, influence, and hold each other accountable. The Path to Action model was first introduced in *Crucial Conversations* (2002).

18. **Fundamental Attribution Error.** This one human failing is the source of a lot of human misery. To reduce its impact, all we need to do is imagine ourselves in the other person's situation. Here's a fun article by Mark Sherman "Why We Don't Give Each Other a Break" http://www.psychologytoday.com/blog/real-men-dont-write-blogs/201406/why-we-dont-give-each-other-break

19. **Fear based reactions.** If you're human—and most of us are—some of the best information on how to handle your own emotions is in *The Happiness Trap: How to Stop Struggling and Start Living* (2008). Russ Harris reveals how we tend to have unreasonable expectations about how we "should" feel, and then get caught in our own struggles like a net that tightens the more we fight. Even more fun—really!—is *The Illustrated Happiness Trap* (2013), again by Russ Harris with great little illustrations by Bev Aisbett that mainlined the information straight into my brain.

20. **Lizard brain defense mechanisms.** A key part of our survival system is our amygdalae, or lizard brain, which influences decision-making, memory, and emotional reactions. It kicks in hard when you feel threatened—think "fight or flight" reactions. Seth Godin has written about the lizard brain for some time, including how to get past it in my favorite *Linchpin: Are You Indispensable?* (2011) Seth jam-packed this book with perspective-shifting ideas and applicable nuggets.

21. **The Halo Effect.** Wikipedia has the story of how this tendency to bias results was discovered by researcher Edward Thorndike in the 1920s, and the many realms in which it shows up. http://en.wikipedia.org/wiki/Halo_effect

22. **Shared understanding and working together fully.** The Arbinger Institute put together a real gem with *Leadership and Self-Deception:*

Getting Out of the Box (2002, 2010). While the title is a bit off-putting, the book does a beautiful job helping leaders self-diagnose their own shortfalls as leaders, and provides relatively simple methods to get yourself and others "out of the box" we put ourselves in.

23. **Internal stories are our default.** A beautiful YouTube movie of David Foster Wallace's 2005 commencement speech "This is Water" at Kenyon College illustrates this perfectly: https://www.youtube.com/watch?v=DKYJVV7HuZw

24. **Humanizing Question.** The VitalSmarts guys strike again, from *Crucial Confrontations* (2005), rebranded *Crucial Accountability* (2013). Asking yourself this simple question can often result in finding out what your "story" about the person is. When I hear myself countering, "But this person is not decent / rational / reasonable!" I know where I need to do some work. Another clue is when I hear myself discussing behavior in the absolute: "She never..." "He always..." Real people are rarely that consistent, and I've figured out absolutes mean there's probably a story for me to go work on.

25. **What would our replacement do?** I read about this conversation between Andy Grove and Gordon Moore in *Decisive*, a great book by Chip and Dan Heath (2013). I highly recommend their set of practical tools to ensure your decision making is the best possible. With lots of fun stories and information to boot.

26. **Fixed amount of thinking.** I learned about this at some great training on how to be a better parent offered by the Love and Logic company. On an audio CD *Winning the Homework Battle* (1986), founder Jim Fay relates the following: "Once the kid has decided it's Dad's problem, he's very likely to get into what we call the no sense in both of us worrying about this syndrome. Gee, Dad has that well in hand. I wonder when he's gonna get it straightened out and so on and no sense in both of us worrying about it, right?"

27. **The Bubble Diagram.** Catchy name, no? If you have a better one, just let me know.

28. **Toyota kanban system.** Also called the supermarket method as supermarkets in Japan would use kanban cards with product information on them to request restocking. It was simple brilliance to apply this method to manufacturing. More information at Toyota's website http://www.toyota-global.com/company/vision_philosophy/ toyota_production_system/just-in-time.html

29. **Theory of Constraints (TOC)**. The basic idea of TOC is that every system is constrained somewhere, and by finding and eliminating each constraint, we can get greater throughput, effectiveness and efficiency. The Wikipedia article is a bit technical, yet it can assist the curious in learning more: http://en.wikipedia.org/wiki/Theory_of_constraints

30. **Tyranny of OR, Genius of AND.** In the classic *Built to Last: Successful Habits of Visionary Companies* (1994, 2004), Jim Collins and Jerry Porras surface this shift in approach: are we trapped by the belief that we have to choose just one of a set of contradictory actions, or can we enable the qualities of each to create a superior, combined option? Since then, Jim Collins went on to write *Good to Great: Why Some Companies Make the Leap...And Others Don't* (2001), introducing concepts of "Getting the right people on the bus" and the Hedgehog Concept of choosing what you are passionate about, can be the best at the world at, and your economic driver (what you can make money doing). Great stuff to frame your leadership thinking.

31. **Reducing professional error.** Atul Gawande created *The Checklist Manifesto* (2009) to positively advocate for the use of checklists in important situations like surgery. While I don't know many doctors, I do know highly-professional pilots with literally decades of flying time who religiously go through checklists every time they fly. There's no better test for the effectiveness of a tool than willingly trusting your life to it. Reminds me of the joke about the difference between involvement and commitment—for a breakfast of scrambled eggs and bacon, the chicken is involved and the pig is committed. Surgeons are involved when they use a checklist, yet onboard pilots are by role automatically committed to a safe outcome.

32. **Force field diagram.** This tool is great for analyzing what could be holding you back—and remember that those aren't always negative things but could be positive benefits of not taking action. A valuable resource on the web is Mind Tools, which has this tool among many. http://www.mindtools.com/pages/article/newTED_06.htm

33. **A sampling of process improvement methodologies:** Lean Manufacturing makes "obvious what adds value by reducing everything else" http://en.wikipedia.org/wiki/Lean_manufacturing; Six Sigma "seeks to improve the quality of process outputs by identifying and removing the causes of defects (errors) and minimizing variability" http://en.wikipedia.org/wiki/Six_Sigma; Business Process Improvement "is a systematic approach to help an organization optimize its underlying processes to achieve more efficient results" http://en.wikipedia.org/wiki/Business_process_improvement ; Management by Objectives (defined by Peter Drucker in 1954) "is a process of defining objectives within an organization so that management and employees agree to the objectives and understand what they need to do in the organization in order to achieve them" http://en.wikipedia.org/wiki/Management_by_objectives; and Lean Six Sigma which combines Lean Manufacturing and Six Sigma process improvement to eliminate waste http://en.wikipedia.org/wiki/Lean_Six_Sigma.

34. **System responsibility.** In *Out of the Crisis* (1989) W. Edwards Deming wrote: "I should estimate that in my experience most troubles and most possibilities for improvement add up to the proportions something like this: 94% belongs to the system (responsibility of management), 6% special." As organizations flatten, I believe leaders must enable everyone to change the system to get better results.

35. **Feedback loops.** Very cool Wired Magazine article on how feedback loops can help us be our best at http://www.wired.com/magazine/2011/06/ff_feedbackloop/

36. **Defeated by the system.** I did get to the central office and close the account. A follow-up letter to the bank president offering my help

to improve their systems for their people and customers remains unanswered.

37. **Loss Aversion.** In *The Personal MBA* (2010), Josh Kaufman collected the best ideas from thousands of books and research studies to create a brilliant compilation of virtually every concept needed to understand and succeed as a businessperson. One of those concepts is Loss Aversion, the fact that people are more driven by what they might lose than by what they might gain. Which explains why I find myself making purchases at the very end of a sales promotion because I don't want to "lose" the discount!

38. **Pareto Principle**. Where else can you learn about an early 20th century Italian economist who gardened? http://en.wikipedia.org/wiki/Pareto_principle

39. **Six Critical Questions.** These come from the second discipline spelled out in *The Advantage*, Patrick Lencioni's 2012 non-fiction summary of the best principles of his work. Pat's created a simple and effective structure of four key disciplines: team alignment, organizational clarity, communication, and reinforcement. I'm a big fan of Pat's practical and effective methods for helping organizations get better.

40. **The fruitless search for certainty and perfection.** I wrote this blog post a few years ago after noticing a pattern, especially in technologically-oriented companies, of looking for the perfect answer that would guarantee results. I believe that this perspective not only wastes time, it harms companies and people by continually sending a message that we can't be good enough—ever. http://trebuchetgroup.com/chris-blog/2013/1/21/the-fruitless-search-for-certainty-and-perfection.html

41. **Minimum Viable Offer.** Another gem from Josh Kaufman's *The Personal MBA* treasure chest. He defines it as "a Prototype that people are willing to purchase." Getting a prototype out into the real world allows you to get real customer feedback to figure out what works and what you really need to improve. It's one thing for potential clients to

share their thoughts on ideas—and it's quite another to get hands-on feedback from using your product or service in the real world.

40. **SouthWest learns from NASCAR.** This is from a simple and effective article on benchmarking entitled, surprisingly enough, as "Benchmarking" by Alan Stratton at his website: http://www.costmatters.com/180-perspective/benchmarking/

41. **Learning Organization.** Peter Senge, in *The Fifth Discipline* (1990), defines a learning organization as living out five main characteristics: systems thinking, personal mastery, mental models, a shared vision, and team learning. A good reference article is at http://en.wikipedia.org/wiki/Learning_organization. At Trebuchet Group, we continue to work toward being a learning organization to both reap the benefits and to be one model for our clients to learn from.

About the author

To Chris, living is about high tech tools and low tech lifestyles. Teams and individuals. Courage and consideration. Exercise and chocolate.

After years of building Legos® and treehouses around the world, Chris went to school for a Mechanical Engineering degree and a Masters in Business Administration. His experiences in the military and the corporate world taught him that great leadership can be learned, and that everyone is a leader.

Chris wants to help create a world where people care for and respect themselves, each other, and the environment. To do so he believes we must inspire businesses to be a greater positive force in the world. His calling is to model, teach, and support businesses and people to be that positive force.

For more information and support on **how to put these principles and practices into action**, please contact a Trebuchet Group consultant at: trebuchetgroup.com.